The Image of God

2-8-03
Carol,
Enjoy the
discovery of
God's Image
in you! Amag
We enjoyed being
with you this weekend!
Love in Christ
Martha

"God's Little Girls Grow Up!"

By Dixie Land Grimes

with

Martha Land Young

Always
remember
that you are
the Image
of God.
Reflect His love
and light to
all around
you
Love Dixie

The Image of God

Reverend Dixie Land Grimes
With
Martha Land Grimes

Copyright 1998
All Rights Reserved

Much, Much More
Reverend Dixie Land Grimes
2755 Wintergreen Court
Phenix City, Alabama
(334) 291-9884
E-mail: angelscry2@msn.com

Martha Land Young
7207 Holland Place NW
Lawrenceville, GA 30043
(678) 985-1844
E-mail: MarthaLand@aol.com

SECOND PRINTING, Expanded

Published By:
Brentwood Christian Press
4000 Beallwood Avenue
Columbus, Georgia 31904

Geneva Queen

Spiritual sister, friend, encourager, supporter,
ennobler, steadfast visionary who
exemplified gentle strength in the beauty of holiness.
Geneva invited us to present at the
North Main Women's Retreat in 1998
for which _The Image of God_ was written.

Peggie Elliott

A bright morning star, Peggie radiates God's love
and the light of Christ to all around her. She and
Geneva caught our vision for a Women's Retreat for
North Main Baptist Church in Danville, Virginia,
in 1984. Through the power of the Holy Spirit, they
multiplied the vision to reach out and touch
thousands of women for Christ.

Peggie, filled to overflowing with the joy of the Lord,
is our spiritual sister and an incredible prayer warrior
for Martha and me.

We lovingly dedicate this edition to the memory of
Geneva Queen and in honor of Peggie Elliott.

Dedicated With Love

The Image of God is lovingly dedicated to my family:

There abideth faith, hope and love,
But the greatest of these if love. _I Corinthians_
_13:13_

The faith and hope of my family gave me the courage and strength to take this first step to share my walk so others can know the Truth that will set them free. Their love goes before me, behind me and surrounds me. My faith, my hope and my love as well as my deepest gratitude goes out to each one of them who is such an integral part of me, my life and _The Image of God._

- Martha - we are One - there is _Much, Much More!_

- Ronnie - my brother-in-law and brother-in Christ - who supports, encourages and makes a way for Martha and me.

- My niece, Christan, her husband, Frank, and her precious triplets: Adam, Jack and Elizabeth, whose very lives are evidence of God's miraculous love. Christan's strength and her unrelenting faith have been awe-inspiring. I am proud of you, Christan.

4

- My niece, Heather, and her husband, Andy, and their adorable son, Connor, whose radiant face brings joy to all around him.
- Jim, my nephew, who brought the Enneagram into our lives. Thank you, Jim, for all you are to me.
- My niece, Kimie, and her husband, Paul, whose respect and admiration are catalysts that keep me running the race.
- Evelyn Land - my physically blind, 90 year old mother, whose belief in me supports me.
- Evelyn Anne - my sister, whose endurance and tolerance of my righteous, reforming personality is awe-inspiring.
- Jim Dixie Land - my father, who is with God ever cheering me on, interceding for me, as he is continuing to provide for his family.
- Mama Omie - my grandmother - whose unconditional love is ever present with me.
- Grace Hassen and Dot Litavecz - my sisters-in-law - who have been there in every way, walking out their love for their brother, Harold - and me. Your mother would be proud of you!
- To Wendee and Allen - my children-in-law - who married into our dynamic family and not only survived but also enhance and enrich all our lives.

- To Laura Compton, Alyson Land, James 'Jay' Gordon, Anna Elizabeth, Jenna Lyn and Jacob Allen - my precious, beautiful grandchildren whose love has been the light of my life! God's love radiates in their eyes and resonates through us as we hold each other. Together we are safe from all life's storms. Dear Ones, you are my heart.

- To my soul mate - Michael J. Trebony - who has become an integral part of my family. God sent him to wake me up! Through his bluntness, tempered with Divine love, he spoke God's Truth that jolted me into reality. Now it is your turn.

- To Dr. Carolyn Harris - my spiritual sister and mirror - who continually points me to the many stories I must tell to be a witness to those coming behind us.

- To Harold - who is walking out of the darkness into the light. With loving kindness, our children and grandchildren have drawn you back to all of us. I am proud of you.

- To Hal, Ben and Dixie Susan - my children - whose love literally carried and still carries me, I dedicate not only this book but also all that I am and ever hope to be. They have been there for their father as well, through the brightest times - and the darkest times. They have turned his heart back to his family - not through trying but through just loving. God's love flowing in and through each one of them has restored the family spiritually and emotionally. I have literally experienced the love of the God of the universe through these incredible human beings! By far, these are the greatest people I have ever or will ever know! They bear witness that God's Divine Image does abide in us! Hal, Ben and Susan, I love you. I respect you. I admire you and I treasure you! May I press ever onward, holding forth the torch until the day I pass it to you!

- Corry, Joy, Colleen, Megan and Peter Finnerty – God's gifts to us. They have been "Jesus with skin on" for our children. They exemplify the Family of God.

In addition, Martha and I celebrate our first book to the cheers of the great multitude of witnesses in our extended spiritual family. Thank you.

- To Dee Dee and Pat Aspell - for their unselfish sharing of their Enneagram materials as well as kindness, patience and professional advice.
- To Don Riso and Russ Hudson - who through their writings, books and tapes have been incredible teachers. They opened the window

of our very souls by revealing the structure and underpinnings of our personalities. But more - much more powerful - has been their example of unconditional acceptance and love as they led the seminars we attended. We are indebted for most of our understanding and sharing of the Enneagram to these self-less, humble, spiritual teachers.

- Robert Lane, my Christian friend and attorney, who stood in the gap and made up a hedge around me during the divorce.

- To Trinity United Methodist Church who never questioned how God was working in and through our lives, but just loved, accepted and supported us where we were in our journey. The choir sang His songs of strength, comfort and joy to me while the congregation strengthened the family with prayer.

- To Dr. Desai - who has been an angel from God to provide the long-awaited psychiatric help for Harold.

- To Michael J. Murphy, M. D., who steadfastly replenishes us with his inspiration, dedication and commitment to God's vision in our lives.

- To the many precious souls in the school systems in Chapin, SC; Danville, VA;

Columbus, GA; and Phenix City, AL. God's voice is not silent in our public schools because of the witness of His Spirit through you!

- To the many saints who are the Body of Christ at Rose Hill Baptist Church, Chapin Baptist Church, North Main Baptist Church, Lakewood Baptist Church and Trinity United Methodist Church.

- The unknown but multitude of dedicated prayer warriors enlisted by Martha in both her church and in her professional walk in Augusta, Georgia.

- To Sandra and Ray Kinsaul - who have given unselfishly of their time, talents, resources and unconditional love and support so that My Songs Given in the Night could be in manuscript form and recorded.

- To the Fourteenth Annual Women's Retreat of North Main Baptist Church - you were the catalyst for our first book, *The Image of God*.

Thank each one of you and all of you for being the outpouring of God's Spirit of Truth and Love for my family and me. We are truly One in the bond of love.

Table of Contents

PREFACE

From the cowardice that dares not face the new truth,
From the laziness that is contented with half-truth,
From the arrogance that thinks it knows all truth.
Good Lord, deliver me. Amen

Prayer from Kenya, Africa

And James and John, the sons of Zebedee, came to
Jesus and said, Master, we want You to do for us
whatever we desire!
And He said, What do you want Me to do for you?
They said, Grant us that we may sit one on Your
right hand, and the other on Your left hand, in Your
glory.
But Jesus said, You know not what you ask; can you
drink of the cup that I drink, or be baptized with
the baptism that I am baptized?
And they said, We can!
And Jesus said to them, You shall indeed drink of
the cup that I drink, and you will be baptized with
the baptism that I am baptized, but to sit on
My right hand and on My left hand is not mine to
give.
Mark 10:35-40

Desire for happiness, achievement and
success sounds goal worthy and innocent enough.

12

But victory and accomplishments do not always bring what we really desire - the peace that passes understanding.

I graduated from high school ranked six in a senior class of 551. I was president of my sorority in college until I quit to get married. Harold, my husband, and I were blessed with three beautiful children. After ten years, I went back to college to complete a BA degree in Music Education. In 1975 I graduated with honors.

I taught music for five years at Chapin Elementary in Chapin, South Carolina, where my children attended school. Harold, my husband, and I became charter members of Chapin Baptist Church which began in the high school chorus room. They called me to be the music director. Our choir rehearsals were held in our living room. Later, the sanctuary was built directly across the road from our home. My sister, Martha, and her family lived next to us.

During that time, the church sent me to a music retreat at White Oak Baptist Center. In actuality, however, I had a Divine appointment. During the stillness of the first night, God's voice pierced through the darkness within a sensation of light, "Music Ministry - Seminary." Immersed in His overwhelming presence, I experienced a peace that passes understanding.

The morning light brought the opposite scenario. In my human frailty, I cried out, "God, You know that I can't follow that directive. I have a husband and three teenagers. I can't just pick them up and go off to the seminary. If that was really You, I expect You to do whatever is necessary to bring it about. Otherwise, I refuse to allow myself to feel guilty about not following it."

During that next year, God did exactly that! Working in and through our lives in dramatic ways, He brought His calling into reality. He did what I could not have done. When I shared this with Chapin Baptist Church, they not only overwhelmingly affirmed and endorsed me, but also financially assisted us with the literal walking out of God's call. In the fall of 1981, my family and I sold our home and acreage and moved to Forth Worth, Texas, where I entered Southwestern Baptist Theological Seminary. Two years later, one of only three girls in my graduating class, I received the Highest Academic Achievement Award. In the fall of 1983, we answered a call to North Main Baptist Church in Danville, Virginia. There I served as Minister of Music and Education for four years. On February

12, 1984, Chapin Baptist Church echoed God's call by ordaining me to the gospel ministry.

Ye have not chosen me, but I have chosen you,
and ordained you, that ye should go and bring forth
fruit, and that your fruit should remain;
that whatsoever
ye shall ask of the Father in my name,
He may give it to you.
John 15: 16

I had been obedient and followed God's leading. Surely He would grant me and my family the peace for which we all longed. But as James and John, I was yet to understand that to truly be in Him I would have to drink of His cup.

To be found in Him... that I may know Him
and the power of His resurrection, and the
fellowship of His suffering, being made
conformable unto His death.
Philippians 3: 9, 10

To the outside world, my life "looked" perfect. I had achieved success and was in a position of honor. This was very true. That was the part of my life I could control. But what the world, and even the few I had allowed to get close to me, didn't know was that mental illness had gripped my husband and was creating a rising tidal wave that would soon come crashing down over us threatening our very lives.

Nor did I understand what was happening right before my eyes. Mental illness is a very closeted disease producing isolation. No one talks about it, because the average person doesn't have a clue to its origins, symptoms, treatments or emotional ramifications on family members. Jokes abound about 'crazy' people. "He's nutty as a fruitcake", "She's got bats in her belfry" and on and on, dot our conversational landscape without a realization of the cruelty of such frivolous remarks. When a loved one is diagnosed with cancer or a host of other understood illnesses, family and friends rally around to offer comfort and support. But mental illness is forbidden territory. Whispers, false information and distancing shroud the deadly family secret, further escalating the disease. Overwhelming fears, very real ones - the loss of jobs, income, insurance, financial security and ridicule, as well as the fear of labeling - paralyze the family. Family secrets - these are the real killers.

By 1985, circumstances around me were so difficult I began to withdraw into my familiar spiritual realm. As I went about my daily activities, I envisioned myself in God's arms, safe and secure. I kept telling myself that I could endure anything if I died to my emotions and personal needs and just lived with Him.

My prayer was, "Lord, let me experience what You felt those three years of your ministry here on earth." Without a doubt, I was God's little girl with an earnest desire to be like Him. Claiming the Scripture, Psalm 37: 3-7, I trusted in the Lord, delighted in Him, committed my way unto Him while I rested in Him. Therefore, He would have to give me the desire of my heart. HE DID! But little did I realize what my desire to experience what he felt entailed.

He was despised and rejected of men; a man of sorrows, acquainted with grief. Isaiah 53: 3

Since that moment, I have struggled daily, hourly - yes, even moment-by-moment - with the walking out of my innocent desire to be like Him. Specifically, for the next three years I struggled in my secret garden while being emotionally crucified.

My prayer today is, "Lord, write and speak through me for Your glory. Knowing the needs of Your children, always hearing the cries of the hurting ones, You feed them with Your words through me. Here am I...use me."

Go now, write it in a book, so that it may be
for the time to come as a witness forever. Though
the Lord may give you the bread of adversity and
the water of affliction, yet your Teacher will not
hide himself,
but your eyes shall see your Teacher.
And when you turn to the right or when you turn
to the left, your ears shall hear a word behind
you, saying, 'This is the way, walk in it.' You will
have a song, as in the night. and gladness of
heart, as when one sets out to the sound of the
flute to go to the mountain of the Lord. And the
Lord will cause His majestic voice to be heard.
Isaiah 30: 8, 9, 20, 21, 30, 31

That same majestic voice draws me with
His everlasting love, reminding me that I was
made in His image:

And God said, 'Let us make man (mankind) *in our*
image, after our likeness. Genesis 1: 26
For I am fearfully and wonderfully made:
marvelous are Thy works. Psalms 139: 14
I (Jesus) *in them, and Thou* (God) *in me,*
that they may be made perfect (mature, grown-up)
in One: and that the world may know that Thou has
sent me and has loved them as You have loved me.
John 17: 23

18

His plans for me and you:

I know the thoughts I think toward you, saith the
Lord, thoughts of peace and not of evil,
to give you an expected end. Jeremiah 29: 11

My testimony, my witness of His Spirit remains:

I waited patiently for the Lord; and He inclined
unto me, and heard my cry. He brought me up also
out of an horrible pit, out of the miry clay, and set
my feet upon a rock, and established my goings.
Psalms 40: 1, 2

I am finally ready, willing and able to share my journey to re-discover and develop His Divine Image in me! Come with me, the best is yet to be - the last for which the first was experienced.

Chapter 1

<u>The Beginning</u>

"Since People Are Pearls Of Great Price,
Our Path Must Be Personal."

For fifty years, I was a prisoner of my own fears, anger and self-criticism, personally walled off in an emotional castle constructed of impenetrable defense systems, surrounded by a mote filled with piranha. When I sensed conflict or felt threatened, I would either withdraw from or attack with a sharp word or a cold look - complete with a raised eyebrow - anyone that dared come too close. Outward appearances manifested strength and control, yet inside I was shrouded with fear, self-doubt and bridled anger.

> *Searching for direction,*
> *Which way should I go?*
> *Can anyone show me?*
> *Does anybody know?[1]*

Early in life as vulnerable children, Martha, my younger sister, and I withdrew from difficult situations over which we had no control. We would go into our shared bedroom and create our own

---

[1] Grimes, Dixie Land. "Living From the Inside", 1996.

little world where we were safe. We played dressing up, tea party, mama and baby, and school. It is not surprising that I was always the teacher. Martha must have come pre-packaged with patience. Often we pretended to be beautiful movie stars married to handsome leading men. To have each other was a great blessing; however, I began to build emotional walls, brick-by-brick, sealing off my vulnerable inner spirit to shield it from outside hurts. These defense mechanisms became my personality - the image I projected to the world. This emotional castle had a high tower where my personality, complete with inner critic, was born and developed. When I slipped into this self-made tower, I viewed conflict or other perceived hurts from a safe distance. It sounds good, but this carefully erected safe-haven kept me from becoming all He created me to be. This survival strategy became a prison of my own making from which escape seemed impossible. That Divine Image, that aspect of God I was designed to reflect, was the prisoner, and my personality was the jail keeper. Even as an adult, both personally and professionally, at the slightest hint of conflict, I would retreat, refusing to see what was happening right before my eyes. My focus of attention was to be **correct** and **right** - follow God's Way and not stray from His Word. Surely my righteous aspirations would be my family's salvation. That's how I fit into and received worth and value in my original family dynamics. Since my personality served me well in childhood, I continued using its survival strategies as an adult. Criticism was the trigger that would catapult me back into my castle, back into my ivory tower, our childhood room, into a spiritual realm where everything worked out, and I was safe. I was God's little girl, and I expected Him to take care of me as I lived out my life from my ivory tower. Surely He would change all around me and make them love Him as I did. I prayed. I cried. I whined. I searched the Scriptures and claimed every promise. With the saints under the altar, I cried out with a loud voice,

How long, O Lord, holy and true?

Revelation 6: 10

But at 43 years of age, everything in my life was not working out even though I was trying as hard as I could. The tidal wave created by Harold's mental illness crashed down over us. A devastating, life-threatening event in our home

23

caused the splitting of our family. But even then, I could not force Harold to get help. For almost a year the children and I lived in an apartment waiting and hoping for a change. Emotionally and spiritually, I built a way station and there sat and cried unto God, "Where are You? If You don't honor my prayers and heal my husband, and restore my family, my whole life is a joke." How like Elijah as he ran from the criticism of Jezebel. Sitting under a juniper tree, he cried,

It is enough...I have been very jealous
for the Lord God of hosts and I, even I, am left.
I Kings 19: 4, 10

From my way station, I continued to minister to many as they walked along their journey. But I was personally paralyzed by my frustration at God's apparent refusal to honor my request to heal my husband and restore my family. I struggled as to what to do.

The way seems so distant,
And yet so very near.
Questions come to haunt me,
But answers aren't so clear.[2]

The morning of January 1, 1987, I awoke early to see an incredibly beautiful scene outside

---

[2] *Ibid.*

my bedroom window. A blanket of pure white snow covered everything in sight. Immersed once again in the purity of His presence, I heard His magnificent voice, "You will be my Minister of Refuge" - not a leader high and lifted up, wearing a white garment, but one baring in her body the marks of grief and pain, able to empathize with the downtrodden, the souls in the ditches. But I was not ready yet. The battle was still raging on the outside. I did not understand that there was much more to come.

Still determined to fix it, I focused on yet another plan. Maybe in his hometown my husband could regroup, and our lives could be restored. Harold, Susan and I moved to Phenix City, Alabama. Ben, newly married, and Hal, engaged, decided to stay in Danville. Trying to follow the rules, expecting God to honor my efforts, I was wrong again. His words resounded in my mind.

Your thoughts are not my thoughts
or your ways My ways.
Isaiah 55: 8

How true. To my amazement, it was with me that He had another Divine appointment in Phenix City. For two years, apart from the organized church that I loved so dearly, I waited, still and receptive, remembering His words, 'Minister of Refuge'. Like Elijah under the juniper tree, I received nourishment and time to rest in His arms.

And as he lay and slept under a juniper tree, behold, then an angel touched him, and said unto him, 'Arise and eat'.
And he looked, and, behold, there was a cake baked on the coals, and a jar of water at his head. And he did eat and drink and laid him down again.
I Kings 19: 4-6

I continued to experience His truth.
I will never leave you or forsake you.
Hebrews 13: 5

I identified with many of the saints who had gone before me.

Wherefore seeing we also are compassed about with so great a cloud of witnesses, let us lay aside every weight, and the sin which doth so easily beset us, and let us run with patience the race that is set before us. Looking unto Jesus the author and finisher of our faith; who for the joy that was set before Him endured the cross, despising the shame, and is set down at the right hand of the throne of God.
Hebrews 12: 1-3

He was strengthening me in preparation for the next step in my journey. I would be ready to face the next catastrophic event.

In the spring of 1993, our marriage of thirty years crumbled as the realities of my husband's mental illness no longer could be hidden or ignored. Because I still had not faced nor dealt with the problem, it again escalated beyond my control in his work place creating devastating results for all of us. By withdrawing from the fray, I had allowed the situation to intensify beyond repair.

Why have I run so
When I didn't need to roam,
Blocking inner vision
That keeps me from home?
I'm looking for the answers
Screaming as I run.
He calls me to listen,
'The battle has been won.'[3]

Only through letting go of my husband and literally placing him in God's hands, did we both fall into nothingness in order to find everything. It is an awesome thing to fall into the hands of God.

---

[3] *Ibid.*

I saw myself on a precipice - behind me was a pack of rabid wolves racing toward me, seeking to devour me; below me was a deep canyon with a river filled with piranha that seemed to be destined to eat my flesh. Where now, God? Where now? It was again a moment of choice.

From within that darkness, God's answer came. **"Take wings and fly free."**

And I bare you on eagles' wings, and brought
you unto Myself. Exodus 19: 4
But they that wait upon the Lord shall renew
their strength; they shall mount up with wings as
eagles; they shall run, and not be weary; and they
shall walk, and not faint. Isaiah 40: 31

Immediately the weight of the agony fell, and I experienced the ecstasy of letting go. "You are safe in My hand, within My plan." His voice comforted me.

"Forgive me, Lord, but I need confirmation. If You have ever spoken to me through Your Word, speak to me now." I picked up my Bible. It fell open to Ezekiel 12: 3.

Therefore, thou son of man, prepare thee stuff for
removing, and remove by day in their sight.

Totally immersed in Him, I fell into a deep, peaceful sleep.

The next morning there arose within me ter-
rifying thoughts of the consequences of walking out
His revealed answer. Turning again to the scripture
He had given me, His words jumped out:

Eat thy bread with quaking, and drink thy water with
trembling and with carefulness...that her land may
be desolate from all that is there, because of
the violence of all them that dwell therein.

Ezekiel 12: 18, 19, 25

"Yes, Lord, Your way will not be easy, but
in Your Grace, I will walk it out – no matter what
the world says."

Letting go meant divorce, the unpardonable
sin in my eyes. Always, I had endeavored to do what
was right and to follow God's word. I had failed! All
was in shambles. When others came to me broken
and defeated, I told them that His Grace was sufficient. It was so easy to talk the talk, and I really
believed it - for others. David was a deceiver, an adul-
terer, and a murderer. Paul persecuted His church.
Peter denied Him. The woman at the well was a
woman of ill repute yet Jesus never condemned her.
He knew them and with loving-kindness drew them
into Himself and gave them a mission to reach out to
others. But now it was me. Was His Grace sufficient
for me? Yes! For in that Grace, He took my hand

and led me out of my tower, free to be me, all I am designed to be.

I thank Him that I was anchored by my strong belief system, my faith and loved ones who patiently stood by me. Eating the bread of adversity and drinking the water of affliction, I listened to my Teacher, the Holy Spirit, as He showed me the Way. Through the agony of crucifying myself, my personality, I learned to trust Jesus enough to let go and embrace the grace I felt that I had to earn by doing what was right.

Letting Go
It's the Hardest Thing I Know,
But You Won't Grow
Till You Let Go.[4]

With much fear and trembling, I **chose** to let down the drawbridge of my emotional castle. I walked out to face the real enemy, not my mentally ill husband or others who I perceived had hurt me, but myself, my inability to face and deal with problems – physically, emotionally as well as spiritually. By withdrawing from conflicts and always trying to fix the problems instead of confronting situations and dealing with them, I had

---

[4] Grimes, Dixie Land, "Letting Go", 1998.

become an enabler. **The shroud of my personality had kept me from the abundant life!**

I am come that they might have life, and that they might have it more abundantly. John 10: 10

All my trying had left me at the bottom of an emotional heap.

Oh wretched man that I am. Who shall deliver me from this wretched body of death?

Romans 7: 24

Slowly, cautiously, held tightly by Christ, I began to look inward seeking to "know myself" in order to discover why I had allowed many destructive things. Ever present was my Teacher saying, "This is the Way. Walk in it."

I'm opening the door now,
Willing to be free.
He had all the answers
Just waiting there for me.

It's looking on the inside
That I've found the key
That unlocked the prison
I created in me.

Living from the inside
That's where I want to be.

Reaching out to others
Who will find their way through me.
Love is the answer. His Love is the key
Love will tear the walls down
that imprison you and me.[5]

---
[5] Grimes, Dixie Land, "Living From the Inside", 1997.

Chapter 2

The First Garden

"A Biblical Garden Celebration"

As I began to look inward seeking to know myself, God drew me to a closer look at the three gardens in the Bible. God's plan for mankind is beautifully seen from this perspective: the Garden of Eden, the Garden of Gethsemane and the Eternal Garden. To my surprise it also revealed how personalities began and developed. May I invite you to go with me to a Garden Celebration. A revisiting of the Three Biblical Gardens begins with a story about **love** and **loss** and **restoration.** Let's start at the Beginning, the Garden of Eden.

The Eve Story

Once upon a time, there was a beautiful girl. Her name was Eve. She looked just like her father, who loved her with all of His heart. She and her handsome husband, Adam, lived in a lush Garden created just for them. It was beautifully adorned for their pleasure and filled with delicious fruit for their nourishment.

Among the fragrant evergreens and scrubs, there were walnut trees and sweet bay laurels. The first olive trees, that would later symbolize beauty, blessings, strength and prosperity, exemplified the peace of the Garden. This round-headed, abundantly branched tree rose forty feet yielding small white flowers along with green and black berries. Out of massive trunks, the great revered cedar trees reached even higher - a hundred feet - upward to the sky. Very graceful juniper bushes with white sweet-pea scented flowers were much taller than the ground cover of today, providing shade for an afternoon rest.

Almond, pomegranate and fig trees along with raspberries, blackberries and boysenberries delighted all of the senses. 'Sweet cane', mint, cinnamon, and caper berries became the first tastes of dessert. The profusely growing caper berries, running like ivy, spread over much of the ground. By the rivers of water, exquisite lilies grew offering a visual feast of scarlet and white blossoms rising from olive brown bases.

A brilliantly colored array of birds was a splendor to behold: eagles, turtledoves, swallows, cranes, warblers, yellow wagtails and quail, to name a few. As they soared through the trees, rested on the lakes and fed on the rivers of water, their songs were the music of the Garden.

As the sun rose with its scorching heat, the profuse foliage of the Garden acted as a huge canapé, shielding the Divinely created man and woman. Adam and Eve spent every waking moment sharing the splendor of their Garden and enchanted lives. They indeed were special, unique, created by their Father to love and be loved. They enjoyed a rich fellowship in union with Him and each other.

In the cool of the evening, as the sun's rays filtered softly through the trees creating a misty veil, the Father walked and talked with them. The birds sang their joyous songs as the animals playfully scampered around in endless delight. I can imagine Eve fashioning a gorgeous garland of fragrant flowers for her hair.

As Adam and Eve tended and explored their bountiful Garden home, every moment of each day was an adventure. They were experiencing the Divine Present. There were no worries about the past or the future. All was provided. There were no fusses, no fights, no arguments, no criticisms, no 'hurry ups', and no money problems - just sweet communion - Holy Oneness. They hardly knew where they stopped and where He began their union was so complete.

But one day, this beautiful girl was walking alone, delighting in the luscious Garden fruits, enraptured by the magnificence of her surroundings, when she heard an unfamiliar voice.

"What a beautiful Garden. Why doesn't your Father let you eat of every tree here?" The snake slithered around her as he introduced her first negative thought.

"We can eat the fruit of every tree except the one in the middle. God told us that if we eat of that fruit, we will surely die." She replied, struggling to negate the disturbing doubt that was creeping into her mind.

The snake stopped, holding his head up, his eyes meeting hers, "Surely you do not believe that. You will most assuredly not die. In fact, just the opposite will happen. Your eyes will be opened and you and your husband will know everything. You will be as gods and goddesses. You will know as much as your Father!"

Eve heard the voice of deception that had introduced doubt, implying that she didn't know enough, had not been told everything. Maybe God didn't think she was intelligent enough to understand. This new feeling of doubt weighed heavily upon her. She had to find out for herself!

She turned.

The tree in the middle of the Garden was magnificent! Maybe the snake was right. Maybe she didn't know enough. Maybe something was missing, causing her to be inadequate. She experienced fear for the first time. **Fear: F**alse **E**vidence **A**ssumed **R**eal!

Choosing to believe the snake's deceptive voice and following his worldly direction, Eve ate the fruit of the forbidden tree, directly disobeying her Father. As she offered it to Adam and he accepted, they both fell into the world of duality: Good and Evil. A world totally opposite to her beautiful Garden, it was full of clamoring and chaos - the bitter fruit of listening to voices other than God's. She had eaten and tasted of the fruit of the world. A cataclysmic shift occurred as she experienced the moment of separation from the innocent, protective and unconditional love known in the first Garden.

There had been a kernel of truth in the snake's deceptive words. She indeed learned what she had not known before. She now knew disobedience, dishonor, and disgrace - exactly what her Father had shielded her from. The first fruits of this reorientation from the inside to outside were fear and shame resulting in the awareness of naked-ness and vulnerability. She wanted to hide! This first worldly desire for a covering drove her to fashion a garment. Quickly sewing together opaque fig leaves using beautiful vines, she created the first emotional armor to cover the hurt she felt from these terrible new feelings and her perceived separation from the Father's love. This shift resulted in the birth of Ego, or what we call Personality or False Self.

The transparent awareness of Divine Love - Divine Reality - was exchanged for the murky illusions of the world of Ego or False Self.

Their fellowship was broken.

In the cool of the day when God came calling, Adam and Eve were in hiding. "Adam. Where are you?"

"I was afraid because I was ashamed, so I hid myself." Adam replied.

"Who told you to be ashamed? Have you eaten of the tree of knowledge...the one I told you not to touch?" The Father knowingly prodded.

"The lady that You created for me made me do it." He complained.

God turned to Eve and asked, "What have you done?"

"The snake made me do it." She cried, defensively.

Oh, the horror of it! Yet another fruit of disobedience - guilt - made Adam and Eve turn on each other as well as God! The fall from unconditional love was a deadly descent!

No wonder God told them not to eat of the tree in the middle of the Garden. It was the Tree of Knowledge of Good and Evil. It opened up to them the emotional giants of the world that condition us to experience fear, shame, guilt and blame.

So they were driven out of the Garden, from Oneness into the world of a-loneness by making the wrong turn, from looking at and trusting in God, to looking at and responding to the voices of the world. The search to recapture their loss tragically began through the distorted efforts of Ego, or Personalities.[6]

Yes, this is an old story, but it is recreated every moment of every day. It has happened to me. And I venture to say that is has happened to you.

---

[6] Genesis 3, KJV.

God created
man in
His Own
Image...

Genesis 1:27

Chapter 3

Our First Garden

"Innocence Lost"

Just like Eve, in the Beginning, we were created in the Image of God, "fearfully and wonderfully made"[7], the embodiment of unique expressions of the Divine.

And God said, Let Us make man in Our Image, after Our likeness. Genesis 1: 26

Thus we were born pure Spirit, pure awareness, un-conditioned love, adorned with special gifts and qualities of God. We were innocent, questioning not our existence. Aware of no past nor future, we lived in the Divine present, delighting in each unfolding moment as we observed from our inner sanctuary. Coming from the Source of Love, we were connected, whole, at one with the "I Am".

Excitedly, we began to focus outward wanting to be a part of this stimulating, new environment, which was good. But just as Eve in the original Garden scene, we encountered voices.

As young children, we also experienced a gigantic shift in the way we saw and responded to

---

[7] Psalms 139:14.

the world. We heard harsh voices, saw tightened facial expressions, felt tensions in relationships, telling us that we are inadequate that something was wrong with us.

"No, that's not right. What's wrong with you? Are you stupid or something? Stop crying. Leave me alone. You are just like your dad... sister...uncle. You are too young. You are too old. You are inadequate. You will never amount to anything. You are nothing but trouble. You are embarrassing me. You have ruined my life."

Yes, there were and still are devious voices, ever spewing out their venom in our world, as we now see its dark side. The trauma was and still is devastating. We, too, wanted to hide, so we created an emotional armor to cover our vulnerable inner Spirits. The Divine Innocence became a memory.

In order to stop the hurt, we brought into *being* defense systems to cover the hole left by our perceived loss of *un-conditional* love and to cover and to hide, or mask, our real feelings. Once again these maneuvers resulted in a wrong turn, a re-focusing of our attention from the inside to the outside giving birth to our Egos, our Personalities, or False Selves - distortions of our Divine Image. Receiving mixed messages, the Inner Spirit seemed to split, reeling from the loss of support and sudden loud clamor of the outer world resisting separation from love. Paul, in Romans 7[8], passionately writes of this inner split, this internal conflict.

For I delight in the law of God in my inward self, but I see in my members another law at war with the law of my mind, making me captive to the law of sin (separation) that dwells in my members. Wretched man that I am! Who will rescue me from this body of death (Ego or Personality)*? Romans 7: 22-24*

Our quest for a return to wholeness begins. We build our lives seeking ways to avoid feeling the pain of loss by filling the 'holes' with false ideas, beliefs about who we are in response to the deluded, *conditioned* opinions of others. But despite avoidance techniques, we still feel this gnawing emptiness. In truth, our putting on of False Selves, or Personalities, in order to get others to love us cannot create the love we need. It just narrows our perception creating tunnel vision. Hidden agendas and underlying motivations arise, fueled by basic fears and basic desires. We lose sight of our Divine Oneness. In order to cope, we take on a distinct survival strategy, which becomes

---

[8] Romans 7: 14-24.

our Personality, our covering, our mask. We decide that we can get the love and acceptance that we so desperately need, if we become either:

> More Perfect, or
>
> More Helpful, or
>
> More Successful, or
>
> More Romantic, or
>
> More Intellectual, or
>
> More Loyal, or
>
> More Fun-loving, or
>
> More in Control, Stronger, or
>
> More of a Peacemaker.

So we try even harder. The irony is that when we try to get love, worth and value from others around us, by being more perfect, etc., we become defensive. And the more defensive our Personalities become, the more they are doomed to lead us down a dark path. The hurts and the rejections we feel, along with the disappointments we experience, create the perceived fall from Grace - the opposite of what we desire.

Tragically and with devastating results, we look for love in all the wrong places. Alcohol and drug abuse, depression, love of money, power, prestige, lust, greed, materialism and vanity become the fruits of trying to fill up the emptiness, the void, created when we do not allow God to be our Source of Life. With Paul, we cry,

O wretched man that I am! Who will rescue me
from this body of death?

Romans 7: 24

But this is not the end of the story. There is good news. There is a way back! There is the Way, the Truth and the Life! We have already been reclaimed, shown the way back to wholeness as modeled by The Way - Jesus in the second Biblical Garden, the Garden of Gethsemane.

There is therefore now no condemnation for those
who are in Christ Jesus. For the law of the Spirit of
life in Christ Jesus has set you free from the law of
sin and of death.

Romans 8: 1

But before we go to the Second Garden, we - like Paul - must be stopped on *our* 'Damascus Road', blinded to the cares of the world, in order to focus on ourselves physically, emotionally and spiritually. A one-on-one encounter will reveal what created our personal defense systems, our emotional strongholds. Corrected vision is absolutely necessary before we can take our next step.

The Re-Discovery of the Image of God in Ourselves and Others

How much would you pay for a pair of glasses that help you see beyond the façade that other people have built brick by brick?

To understand why they act the way they do and react the way they do.

The most basic and fundamental skills needed for living in our world as the Image of God - understanding self and others - is rarely taught. Any interaction or relationship initially begins with You!

Chapter 4

The Weapons of Our Warfare

"The First Weapon - The Enneagram"

God had the weapons of our warfare for the pulling down of our strongholds and corrected vision ready and waiting for us.

For the weapons of our warfare are not carnal,
but mighty through God to the pulling
down of strongholds;
Casting down imaginations, and every high thing
that exalteth itself against the knowledge of God
and bringing into captivity every thought to the
obedience of Christ... II Corinthians 10: 4, 5

The first weapon was the Enneagram, a study of personalities - a model of awareness – that blends spirituality and psychology. *Ennea* is Greek for nine and *gram* is Greek for point. I discovered it through my nephew, Jim, who had received it from his best friend's parents, Lee and Franklin Brooks. Dr. Brooks was a psychologist in Augusta, Georgia. Although I knew they were strong Christians, I was very skeptical of anything psychological. I researched, read and explored every facet of this incredible personality system. A tool for self-observation, it allows for self-understanding spiritually, physically and emotionally! Unlike other personality systems, it shows not only behavior traits but also specific motivations created by our basic fear leading to our basic desire. It reveals our focus of attention that can narrow our perception making it difficult to understand and/or deal with another person's point of view. The Enneagram provides a way to *let go* of the wretched man that Paul speaks of in Romans 7 - the old nature in each of us - in order to allow the new nature given to us by the sacrifice of Christ to be revealed.

To my surprise, as I began to put some of its principles into practice, IT WORKED! I had always known that there are fundamental personality patterns that effect our beliefs and behaviors; but through the Enneagram, I came face to face with my own personality and how its mechanisms work in and through me! Horror of horrors, I began to see flaws that I had never seen before. Little by little, in the midst of an ongoing, agonizing inner struggle, I began to tear down the strongholds that had bound me.

The process awakened my vulnerable inner spirit and so strengthened me that I began to want to share it with others.

The first stirring of life energized me. I resounded the victorious words of Paul as we both proclaimed:

I (Personality) am crucified with Christ,
nevertheless I (His Divine Image) live; yet not I,
but Christ lives in me; and
the life I now live in the flesh I live by
the faith of the Son of God, who loved me and gave
Himself for me. Galatians 2: 20

Sharing The Enneagram Tool

Because this tool has meant so much to Martha and me, with joy we share it with you. We know - because we have experienced it - one cannot separate body, mind or spirit. We take who we are, all we are, into our homes, our ministry, our churches, our work places and social activities. "Who" we are determines "how" we act. "How we act" is an outer expression of our inner life. Who is in control - our self-created personalities complete with survival strategies and defense systems or our God-created Divine Image mirroring a beautiful aspect and charac-teristic of Jesus Christ, the pearl of great price?

The Kingdom of Heaven is like a merchant man,
seeking goodly pearls: Who, when he found one
pearl of great price, went and sold all that he had,
and bought it. Matthew 13: 45, 46

We must take time to be holy - whole, mature, complete!

We each have a little of all personality traits, but our Egos are centered around a specific focus of attention creating a distinctive image we portray to the world. There is no one personality type that is better than the rest. Read the descriptive paragraphs and decide which best expresses the way you are most of the time - not how you want to be, but how you really are. Being honest with yourself is the first step in re-discovering your Divine Image.

After you have located the number of your personality type, read the Personality Strongholds that follow the quiz. See if you identify with the strongholds that correspond with your type. Truly there is nothing new under the sun.

PERSONALITY QUIZ

This self-assessment quiz describes nine different personality types. None are better or worse than any of the others, but they do see the world differently. Select the description that fits you best. If you find it difficult to choose between two or more of the paragraphs, think about how someone close to you would describe you.

1 - I am a very organized, orderly person. I have a very definite sense of right and wrong, and I don't understand why everyone else does not have the same values. I have strong work ethics and a low tolerance for co-workers who do not. Honesty and integrity are very important to me. It is very difficult for me to relax and be spontaneous. I am always on time for work. Why can't everyone else be? Work always comes before play – if I play at all. Even though I sometimes come across as critical, others are not aware of the fact that I am the most critical of myself. I have unrealistic expectations of myself. I worry constantly about doing the 'right thing'. I love making every detail perfect. When stressed, I become angry and defensive. Most of the time this is because I am angry that others don't understand what pressure I put on myself and how hard I try. You can count on me to perform my job according to the proper policies and procedures. I dread being criticized or judged by others. On the inside I truly desire to make the world a better place. Others may see me as aloof, straitlaced and cool, but I am intensely passionate about my ideals and belief.

2 - Others like me around because of my warm, friendly, caring manner. I feel good being needed, being central in people's lives. I like working with people around me. I need people connection. I tend to define love by doing for others. I am highly responsive to approval and encouragement and crushed by disapproval. I feel that others might not make it unless I'm around. I am the one who takes care of everyone at work – I remember birthdays, anniversaries, etc. Sometimes I get physically ill and emotionally drained from taking care of everyone else. I resent it when others take my caring attitude for granted. I tend to put myself down hoping others will say it isn't true. I must avoid fishing for compliments or doing for others so they will be obligated to be my friend. I am not comfortable being on center stage, but I am very comfortable being the boss's right hand – the power behind the throne. Supporting them in their position of authority. I seem to know what the boss needs before he/she does.

3 - I am image conscious, task oriented, practical, efficient, and assertive. Often, I put my work before relationships. I go full force until I get the job done. Don't waste my time. **I'm on - don't interrupt me!** It is very important to me to be successful in all that I do. I tend to adapt in order to create the impression I want. I can be a workaholic in order to get a project to completion. Failure and rejection make me feel very uncomfortable, and I will go to great lengths to avoid them. I have a lot of energy and enjoy motivating those around me to action! I can 'act' like I know what I am doing when, in fact, I don't have a clue. I am a performer who loves center stage. I like to see results NOW! I am attracted to people who offer me an opportunity for advancement – I am a great networker! To truly grow as a person, I must develop my interior self as well as my "image". When I seek knowledge, 'faking' a certain image is no longer necessary. It is difficult for me to slow down long enough to take a vacation - or to rationalize that it is okay for me to take a vacation.

4 - I am a free spirit, a unique individual who feels intensely about my life, my work and my relationships. I feel deeply and can be empathetic with others, but I do not like to be compared to others. I like distinctive work that utilizes my creativity. I can inspire, influence, and persuade through the arts, the written and spoken word. I find it difficult to maintain interest when I finally get what I have longed for. My focus of attention is on "what's missing in my life. I must be alert to achieving goals without experiencing a let down that it is never enough. I can make an ordinary job interesting as long as I can see the worth of my work. I resonate with people who take the time to understand me. Sometimes people say I'm moody. I have to guard against emotional highs and lows. **Please, God, don't let me be average!**

5 - I am a strategist, a seeker of knowledge, an analyst and theoretician. I have a very active interior world and enjoy gathering data. I get lost in my interests and like to be alone with them for hours. Since I prefer to stand back and observe people, I can come across as aloof and distant. I must have my space in order to think. I am extremely productive when not placed on the front line. Do not approach me with a problem or an idea until you have thoroughly thought it through yourself. Be ready to answer my questions. I must remember that it is important to share my knowledge rather than to look down on other's lack of knowledge.

6 - I am a great team player, loyal to the organization. I like clear lines of authority. I am a very hard worker. Being neat and orderly helps me feel more in control of my life. I am great at circling the wagons to defend against the common enemy. I have the ability to see all potential dangers thereby anticipating problems and developing solutions. One minute I think confidently then the next, insecurely. Doubt can create fear, "It wouldn't work anyway, why try it?" I have to guard against my insecurities causing passive-aggressive behavior. It is critical to know where I stand with my authority figures so I won't waste energy worrying about their motives. I must be thoroughly prepared before I go into any situation. Consumer Report is a great source of information. I need to run my ideas through someone whose opinion I respect.

7 - I am extremely extroverted, spontaneous, fun loving and have many areas of interest. I like to laugh and enjoy interacting with others. I have the ability to create a vision, plan for positive outcomes, and I don't like to look at the negatives. This can place me in denial. I can see limitless possibilities. I am a high-energy go-getter who gets bored with routine. I am good at consulting, motivating and networking but become frustrated when others are negative or don't share my vision. I have problems following through with the details of a project because I am rushing ahead with a new one. I prefer others to bring it to closure. I am uninhibited, witty and blunt; therefore, I have to be careful not to offend. **Tact - What's that?** Fear of boredom can lead to hyperactivity. When there is a problem, I tend to tune it out by creating distractions. There are so many avenues to explore.

8 - I am a strong and powerful person. I am aggressive, forceful and demand respect. I am tough-minded, but I can be very vulnerable with someone I trust. I feel in control when calling the shots and others follow my lead. I work hard and expect others to do the same. I push the limits and will not be manipulated. Trust is a huge issue with me. I am a bold wheeler-dealer and behind the scenes, a consensus builder. I fight for what is right and defend the underdog. I value directness and honesty. I put my cards on the table. I say what I mean and mean what I say and want others to do the same. When I enter a group, I immediately know who the most powerful person is. Do not try to manipulate me. I like a worthy opponent. Confront me head on. I take charge and get the job done! I have to guard against running over people with my energy and powerful nature. I have to guard against being a tyrant rather than a leader.

9 - I seek peace and harmony in all areas of my life. Since peace at any price is my motto, I rarely get angry and will go to all links to avoid a confrontation; but if backed into a corner, I will fight. My ability to see all sides of an issue makes me an excellent peacemaker. I like a predictable environment with clear responsibilities. I adapt very well to people's needs and the organization's goals. I comply with the decisions of others but resist sudden or fast-paced change. People tend to underestimate my abilities because I am not competitive and never call attention to myself. It is difficult for me to generate a lot of energy toward a project. I need to be energized by others. Feedback and support help me. When I am engaged, I am very diligent and extremely productive. Don't tell me what to do or try to control me; just ask and I will be happy to comply. Otherwise, I can become very stubborn, immovable.[9]

[9] Palmer, Helen, and Paul B. Brown. *The Enneagram Advantage.* New York: Harmony Books, 1998.

Personality Strongholds

1 Reasonable, truthful, highly principled, conscientious and concerned about ethical standards. A ONE is extremely self-critical. In competition with self - not others. The ONE can become self-righteous and judgmental. Their focus of attention is living in a world where a sense of inner direction motivates them to strive for perfection. (Paul)

2 Sympathetic, helpful, thoughtful, generous and sincerely concerned for the welfare of others. TWOs like a "warm fuzzy" Christian environment. The TWO's focus their attention on the needs of others - sometimes ignoring their own needs. (Martha, Sister of Lazarus)

3 Adaptable, self-assured, attractive, energetic and ambitious with naturally high self-esteem. Image type - always moving into action. The focus of attention for the THREES goes to tasks, to getting things done. THREES like organized church activities and projects. They can be devious. (Jacob, Joseph)

4 Intuitive, introspective, expressive and self-aware, FOURS are able to freely reveal their feelings and insights. FOURS live in a melodramatic world. Motivated by their emotional needs, the FOUR's focus of attention goes to 'what is missing in their lives'. FOURS like an intense, expressive Spiritual fellowship. (Mary Magdalene, Jeremiah)

5 Concentrated, focused, alert, insightful and extremely curious about the world around them, FIVES move away from people and into their heads. The focus of attention for FIVES lies in minimizing participation while cultivating the sense of being an observer. Their thirst for Spiritual knowledge and understanding motivates them. FIVES like intellectual sermons and in-depth Bible studies. (Zacchaeus)

6 Responsible, trustworthy, forming strong bonds for security. SIXES are fear based - their attention focuses on potential threats. They can become paranoid, defensive. Questioning and doubting, they scan the environment. To be safe and accepted is the SIX's motivation for involvement in the Christian community. (Peter)

7 Busy, fun loving, responsive, excitable and enthusiastic about the endless potentialities of life. High energy. They always have ten balls in the air. SEVENS are focused on future plans and pleasant options. A love of ideas and possibilities motivates a SEVEN to want to initiate and participate in Christian activities. They like an open Christian environment. They can be impulsive. (Women at the Well, St. Francis of Assisi)

8 Self-confident, strong, assertive, decisive and authoritative, they take the initiative to make things happen. The EIGHT's focus of attention is control. Self-empowerment coupled with a need to know is their motivation for Spiritual leadership. They can be dominating and combative. (David)

9 Trusting, unpretentious, patient, nonconfrontational, NINES forget themselves and go to sleep. Must be engaged. The NINE's focus of attention is the agenda of others. Motivated and energized from outside. NINES need an interactive Christian environment that keeps them connected. (Man at the Pool, John)

Did you identify with the strongholds of your personality type? Now it is easier to see why there might be some differences of opinion in a group of differing personalities. Remember each type, or personality, is covering a Divine Aspect, a Divine Image, that is seen dimly as through a veil. Read on, still focusing on yourself. This is a one-on-one adventure - our 'Damascus Road' experience.

Appreciates

9 - Stability, patience, peace

8 - Self-Confidence,
respect,
trust

1 - Competence,
quality,
principles

7 – Optimism,
pleasure
versatility

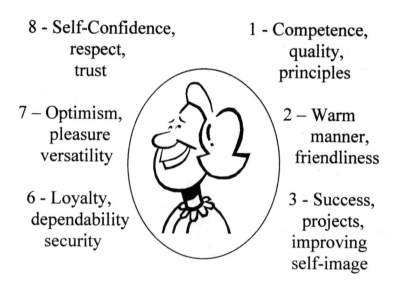

2 – Warm
manner,
friendliness

6 - Loyalty,
dependability
security

3 - Success,
projects,
improving
self-image

5 - Intelligence,
observation,
analysis

4 - Sensitivity,
uniqueness,
intensive feelings

There are circumstances or environments in which we are very comfortable and experience very little stress. In these situations we use our defense mechanisms at a minimum. Here we can be easy to get along with.

Dislikes

9 - Change, arguments, confrontation

8 - Disrespect,
restrictions
untrustworthiness

1 - Dishonesty,
not following the
rules,
irresponsibility

7 – Boredom,
routine,
limits
unfriendliness,

2 - Impersonal
response,

6 - Unreliability
dependability,
unclear lines
of authority

3 - Failure,
inefficiency,
failure,
rejection

5 - Emotional response,
confused thinking
rambling on

4 - Insensitivity,
ordinariness,
blending in

Whether we are aware of it or not, there are many situations
we don't like. These circumstances create resisting energy
within us, and we either act out, eat it or reveal it through
body language. Others see it whether we realize it or not.

Irritating Ministry Styles

Our Personalities become our ministry styles. Sometimes these styles can irritate others. Horror of horrors, we're usually the last person to realize it! Furthermore, people may complain about us behind our backs creating more walls and division.

1   Judgmental; right/wrong; black/white; no mercy and no grace.

2   Hovering; meddling; doing for others in order to be appreciated.

3   Self-promoting; serving in order to improve their image; "Look at me!"

4   Melodramatic; ministry takes on a soap opera or victim mentality; "Woe is me!" "Poor me."

5   Reclusive; withdrawn; choose to withdraw into a world of study without sharing knowledge.

6   Fear of consequences brings about passive-aggressive behavior; expects the worst to happen in all situations.

7   Smart mouthed; unbridled tongue; unfocused; goes from one ministry/church to another.

8   Tyrant; my way or the highway; "I will be in charge of all programs/projects."

9   Passive; avoids conflict at all costs; refuses to speak out for their beliefs.

Wholeness Through The Trinity

God - The Holy Spirit
The Instinctive

God the Father   God The Son
The Head   The Heart

The Enneagram Centers

Instinctive Center
(8,9,1)

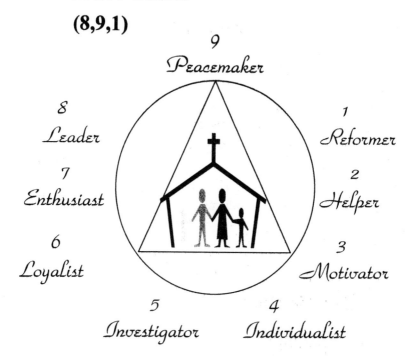

9
Peacemaker

8
Leader

1
Reformer

7
Enthusiast

2
Helper

6
Loyalist

3
Motivator

5
Investigator

4
Individualist

Head Center
(5,6,7)

Heart Center
(2,3,4)

Some people come from a Heart perspective.
Some people come from a Head perspective.
Some people come from an Instinctive perspective.

The Enneagram Centers

Head (5,6,7)

Heart (2,3,4)

Instinctive (8,9,1)

As Leonardo DiVinci portrayed man, we see he is head, heart and instinct (body). We indeed are the mirrors of the Image of the Trinity.

The Heart Center - Two, Three, Four

Events or people energize them as they sense other people's feelings and respond to them. They *need connection* to keep the energy flowing. They may substitute actions for feelings. They are called image types because how others see them is of utmost importance to them. In order to make a decision they compare and contrast. "Which do I like better? Which is more important or has a bigger payoff?" They know right away; therefore, their decisions come very quickly.

Emotional issue - Anxiety.

Head Center - Five, Six, Seven

They are **energized by outside information** - more input. They put their trust in ideas. Concepts and information is key here. They are constantly scanning the environment for clues. Types in this center like to analyze, to take a problem apart and look at its component parts to see how they fit together. These three types make decisions by trying to understand the problem. Everything goes through thought processes first.

Emotional issue - Fear.

The Instinctive Center- Eight, Nine, One

Energy comes from inside - gut level. They have strong wills and control issues. "Whose will is more powerful, yours or mine?" "Who is in control?" "Can I trust that authority?" They hold their ground. Trust their judgment. They make decisions by comparing with a precedent. "Have we done that before?" "Did it work?" "Is this being done successfully elsewhere?"

Emotional issue - Anger

KNOCK
"Chooses To Act" 8,9,1
The will responds by
expressing itself.

**The
Kingdom
of God
-
Wholehearted
Faith
Luke 11:9**

SEEK
"Receives" 5,6,7
Intellect
collects, explores,
analyzes as it
receives.

ASK
"Responds" 2,3,4
Emotion
creates desire
to reach out.

As we were created in His Image for fellowship, the Father woos us to prayerful intercession with Him. Modeled by the Trinity, He provides three basic ways for us to interact with Him through our Centers.

The Heart Center seeks out connection with the Father.

The Head Center asks for knowledge of the Father.

The Instinctive Center interacts with the Father through the will.

The church, the Body of Christ, reflects the Trinity as it Seeks, Acts and Knocks.

NOTES

Will
"Action"
Matthew 28:18-20

**The
Will of
God
John 4:34-38**

I Seek
"Knowledge"
Matthew 6:33

I Desire
"Emotion"
Matthew 22:37-39

"The fields are ripe unto harvest." John 4: 35-38. As He created us in His image, so He gives us different ways to labor in His Kingdom. As the Trinity, God calls us to labor with Him through the uniqueness of our Centers - some through our Emotions, some our Minds, and some through our Wills.

The Imitation of Life

In our own efforts to find worth, value, security and/or satisfaction, we hide behind our self-centered Egos.

1 Paul sought value through correctness, even to the extent of killing innocent people.
2 Martha sought worth through meeting the needs of everyone else, leaving her feeling like a martyr.
3 To receive the family blessing, Jacob deceived his father and brother.
4 Mary Magdalene was totally consumed by demons - raging emotions.
5 Zacchaeus, a Publican, collected revenues for Rome, bringing riches to himself by burdening his own people.
6 Peter, afraid for his life, denied Christ.
7 The Woman at the Well had gone from one man to another seeking fulfillment.
8 David used his power and control to satisfy selfish desires including the murder of an innocent man.
9 The Impotent Man at the pool used his infirmity to keep him from engaging in the process of going to the healing waters.

The Imitation of Life

"What Am I Worth? What Do I Hide Behind?

9 Compliance Man at the Pool
John 5:29

8 Control David
II Samuel 12:1-13

1 Correctness Paul
Acts 9:1-43; 22:3-5

7 Daring
Woman at
the Well
John 4:6-43

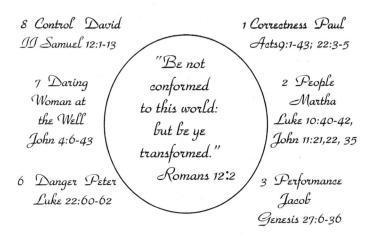

"Be not
conformed
to this world:
but be ye
transformed."

Romans 12:2

2 People
Martha
Luke 10:40-42,
John 11:21,22, 35

6 Danger Peter
Luke 22:60-62

3 Performance
Jacob
Genesis 27:6-36

5 Data Zacchaeus
Luke 19:2-10

4 Personal Mary
Magdalene
Luke 8:2

The Divine Image
Where do I find value?
"Living From the Inside Is Where I Want to Be"

We find true worth and value when we pull down the strongholds of Egos, our Personalities, and become the aspect of Christ that God created us to be. Energized by His Spirit, the Body of Christ is a mirror of the Trinity.

1 Paul transformed into God's Light to the Gentiles.
2 Mary transformed into unconditional love, the Bread of Life, providing nourishment to a hungry world.
3 Jacob transformed into Israel through which Living Water would flow to a dry and parched world.
4 Mary Magdalene transformed into the selfless Way of Christ.
5 Zacchaeus released his fortune as he transformed into the liberating Truth of salvation.
6 Peter transformed into the Door to service via Christ's love and forgiveness.
7 The Woman at the well transformed into the bearer of the Life through the sharing of the first universal call.
8 David transformed as God's Shepherd after God's own heart.
9 The Impotent Man transformed into the Vine as he rose up and walked with the power of faith flowing through him.

The Divine Image

Where do I find value?
"Living From the Inside Is Where I Want to Be"

9 John 15:5 - The Vine

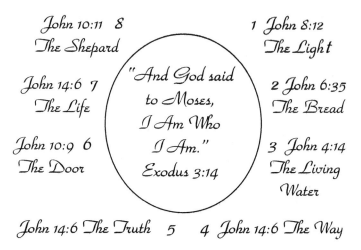

John 10:11 8
The Shepard

1 John 8:12
The Light

John 14:6 7
The Life

"And God said
to Moses,
I Am Who
I Am."
Exodus 3:14

2 John 6:35
The Bread

John 10:9 6
The Door

3 John 4:14
The Living
Water

John 14:6 The Truth 5   4 John 14:6 The Way

We with unveiled faces are being transformed from glory to glory. Born to reflect God's image, we quickly forget as we encounter the world. We put on our covering and take on guilt over the past, anxiousness over the present and fear of the future. We project our vice - the fruit of resisting. Our resulting fixation becomes our Ego image that we portray to the world. Only through the letting go to the pulling down of the strongholds of Ego can we reflect our virtue - our Divine Image, the Spirit of Truth revealed.

The Abundant Life
John 10:10

9 Peace

Meekness 8

1 Joy

Temperance 7

2 Love

Faithfulness 6

3 Goodness

Gentleness 5

4 Long-Suffering

*But the fruit of the Spirit is love, joy, peace,
longsuffering, gentleness, goodness, faith, meekness,
temperance: against such there is no law.*
Galatians 5:22,23

When we abide in Christ, the Spirit of Truth, we become the fruit. Abiding requires no work, no effort - just letting go of any other attachments in order to receive the nourishment of Christ. "I am the true vine and my Father, the husbandman. Abide in Me and I in you." John 14: 1, 3.

What flows through the Vine? What keeps us connected so we can bear more fruit for the Kingdom? Love. "As the Father has loved me, so have I loved you; continue (live) in my love." John 14: 9.

Five ways to enhance your ministry style if you are a/an:

TWO

- Shift your sights from the outside to the inside - discover the unique talents and abilities God has given you. Do not weigh how much you are loved by how much you do for others.
- Allow yourself time to discover your own needs and God's plan for you.
- Believe in your own genuine value as a person. You are fearfully and wonderfully made - God's creation. Be grateful for who you are - do not seek gratitude from others for what you do.
- Balance your helpful nature with a disciplined focus on God's will in your life. You must take care of yourself in order to be able to care for others. "Your body is the temple of the Holy Spirit." I Corinthians 6:19
- Affirm your self-image with positive self-talk such as: "I am caring and helpful." or "I am supportive and giving.".

THREE

- Expand your spiritual vision beyond personal and career advancement to include the whole picture - look at your Christian life as a part of the whole body.

- Develop the supportive side of your nature by acknowledging, complimenting, and promoting the special talents of other Christians and individuals you come in contact with each day.
- Foster a team *esprit de corps*, which values collaboration and rewards loyalty.
- Motivate others to be more encouraging and supportive of each other rather than competitive.
- Balance your passion for achievement with a sensitivity that respects the limits of others.

FOUR

- Stabilize your personal and leadership style by acting on goals and vision rather than reacting to feelings and emotions.
- Follow clear standards and principles so decisions can be made with deliberation rather than impulsiveness.
- Balance your empathy for others' personal feelings with disciplined thinking about the pros and cons for a project and plan within the Body.
- Set specific results you want to attain and spell out clearly each step that is useful to obtain your desired outcomes.

- Overcome the tendency to withdraw in the face of hard realities to a world of fantasy by taking action toward accomplishing tasks.

FIVE:

- Balance your rational analysis of problems with a sensitive perception of peoples' feelings and the impact of issues on individuals.
- Be open to the your feelings as well as your intelligence as sources of information about projects and persons.
- Risk putting your ideas into action and sharing your vision with others so they can benefit from your wealth of insights.
- Learn to assert yourself with enthusiasm and develop confidence in your actions to get an effective response from others.
- Encourage thinking within the Body of Christ by inviting an exchange of ideas and implementing a collaborative approach to solving problems.

SIX:

- Acknowledge whatever real fears and apprehensions you may have about your leadership abilities, remembering that fears are intended to be a servant to inform your thinking and energize your actions, not a ruler to control you.

- Remember: If you fear something could go wrong in the organization, you may be right, and that's worth knowing.
- Break through negative, anxious thinking that could overwhelm you to positive, exciting ideas about all the possibly good outcomes. "Perfect love casts out fear." "I know the plans for you, declares the Lord, plans for welfare and not for calamity to give your a future and a hope." Jeremiah 29:11
- Develop your inner strength with positive self-affirmations such as, "I am sure of my abilities," or "I am confident of my views," or "I trust in my decisions."
- When threatened, do not take the heavy- handed approach to establish your authority.
- Be honest. Always be consistent in your statements in every arena. Others in the organization compare notes.

SEVEN

- Look beyond instant payoffs to discover what is good for the Body in the long run.
- Moderate your enthusiasm for many projects by

focusing your energies on completing a few tasks at a time. The key word is "complete" before taking off on a new task.

- Deepen your appreciation of your leadership by taking time to honor commitments, face unpleasant issues, and put closure on projects.
- Motivate others with your enthusiasm to become a team by finding satisfaction in cooperating with the group on new ventures.
- Balance your creative brainstorming and innovation with practical, realistic steps for completing each project.

EIGHT

- Balance 'the caring for power' with 'the power of caring', helping, and inspiring others so authority can be a tool of service rather than of domination.
- Be sensitive to how strongly you come across to others so your aggressiveness does not create a climate of fear.
- Use your natural gift of leadership reasonably and responsibly to accomplish great deeds and gain the heartfelt respect of others.
- Harmonize your independence and self-determination with reliance on the talents and abilities of others.

- Learn the value of harmony by mediating opposing views and reaching mutually agreed upon conclusions rather than imposing your solutions on problems.

NINE

- Draw on your inner strength to confront difficulties and reconcile differences with others.
- Sacrifice a passing peace to face the hard reality of conflicts and work them through to a lasting peace.
- Learn to be assertive in stating your own views and plans without over-accommodating others' interests.
- Be proactive in setting clear goals and following up with action to get results.
- Prioritize desired results to simplify decision-making and manage changes in a smooth way.

ONE

- Keep a positive attitude - Look on the bright side of tasks and the talents of others.
- Acknowledge your anger towards others and express it appropriately with constructive criticism.
- Break through rigid rules and regulations by

brainstorming without immediately rejecting other's ideas because of their shortcomings. The Love of the Lord rather than the letter of the law.

- Balance the right procedure with genuine concerns for others; balance standard rules with flexible and creative application of principles.
- Be patient with your own development. Perfection should be more of a process than a product. Perfection should be more of a coming to be than an accomplished fact.
- Tell that Ego who demands you to be perfect to "shut up" every once and a while!

Much,

Much

More

Motivated, Mobilized

for

Much, Much More

Chapter 5

The Second Weapon

"Much, Much More"

The second weapon came two years later.

Just as God did not send Moses alone unto Pharaoh (Exodus 4:14-16), but called his brother, Aaron, to go with him to strengthen, undergird and speak for him, God called my sister, Martha to walk with me. Since early childhood, our lives have intertwined. She was always there when I needed her. After my three precious children, Hal, Ben and Susan, were born, God told me to return to college to complete my music degree. But leaving them with a stranger was out of the question for me. During a visit with Martha and Ronnie in our home in Savannah, Georgia, I shared my dilemma with her. Without hesitation, she replied, "I'll keep them." We moved on that Divine offer! God never calls you to do anything without providing the Way.

My family relocated in Columbia, South Carolina, where Martha and Ronnie lived. During that following year, we bought acreage in Chapin, South Carolina, cut out a huge hole in the woods and built houses side by side. It was our piece of heaven where we raised our six children. She kept all of them while I commuted to the University of South Carolina to complete the next step in God's design for me. There are many stories yet to tell about that special place, and that book will come soon. But for now, it is important to know that Martha and I were extremely close, and God set us apart in order to use this time to provide a foundation for the mission He would ultimately give us.

In order to connect the events between our adventure in the woods to the giving of the next tool, you will recall that from Chapin, God sent me to Southwestern Baptist Theological Seminary, in Fort Worth, Texas; then to North Main Baptist Church, in Danville, Virginia; then to Trinity United Methodist Church in Phenix City, Alabama.

While living in Phenix City, I was the choral and drama director at Columbus High School, the liberal arts magnet in Columbus, Georgia - just across the Chattahoochee River.

In actuality, however, He did not send me specifically to these places but **to His saints He had placed there,** divinely equipped to stand in the gap and make up the hedge at each way station along my path. First and foremost, my family stood behind and beside me as I struggled. My mother, daddy and sister, Evelyn Anne, prayed without ceasing - for that is all I would allow them to do. In addition, there were many saints - whose names I do not know - who were directly involved in God's plan for Martha and me. They were the prayer warriors enlisted by Martha in her church, as well as saints in her professional life who made it possible for her to be with my children and me during critical times. And there were specific soul mates placed along the way who, one-on-one, gave a witness to God's Spirit of Truth. Never take lightly your role as a prayer warrior. Not only is it beautiful privilege but also an awesome responsibility.

And I sought for a man among them, that should make up the hedge, and stand in the gap before me for the land, that I should not destroy it. Ezekiel 22: 30

You know who you are - you are the great cloud of witnesses spoken of in Hebrews 12:1. I take this opportunity to say thank you for **Being** His instrument, not only in my life but also to all others God sends to you. As God sent Ananias to minister to Paul, You answered His call to pick up His little girl, Dixie, as she stumbled along her way - blinded to what was happening all around her.

And the Lord said unto him, Arise, and go into the

street which is called Straight, and inquire in the
house of Judas for one called Saul, of Tarsus: for,
behold, he is praying,

Then Ananias answered, Lord, I have heard by
many of this man, how much evil he has done to the
saints at Jerusalem. And here he has authority from
the chief priests to bind all that call on Your name.
But the Lord said unto him, Go your way: for he is
a chosen vessel unto me, to bear my name before
the Gentiles, and kings, and the children of Israel:
For I will show him how great things
he must suffer for My name's sake.

And Ananias went his way, and entered into the
house; and putting his hands on him said, Brother
Saul, the Lord, even Jesus, that appeared unto you
in the way as you came, has sent me, that you might
receive your sight, and be filled with the Holy
Ghost. Acts: 9: 11-17

Yes, I lived in a spiritual realm, but He knew that I needed Jesus with skin on. I found Him, not in organizations, but in the frailty of human form – the true Body of Christ. Each one of you radiated an aspect of Jesus Christ: Meekness, Unconditional Love, Goodness, Long-Suffering, Gentleness, Faithfulness, Joy, Temperance and Peace. (Galatians 5: 22)

God provided the fruits of His Spirit walked out in the flesh of His present day saints. What a contrast from the deceptive fruit of the world as symbolized by the apple in the First Garden.

Using the second weapon, God would bond Martha and me in a new way that would connect every facet of our lives. We would literally begin to walk, talk and experience One Way, together - personally, spiritually and professionally. During the years we lived side by side in the woods in Chapin, God was preparing us for yet another step. In a dramatic Divine intervention, He called us and gave us His vision, His words and His Mission for Act Three of our lives.

This transforming day was May 26, 1995.

I was directing a skit for AFLAC's 40th anniversary held in the Three Arts Theatre in Columbus, Georgia. AFLAC is a local insurance company started by three brothers with a dream to provide affordable insurance for the families of Georgia. This dream has grown to international proportions. Playing to a standing room only audience of employees, my drama students portrayed the initial planning, envisioning session of the brothers. I was thrilled as I saw re-enacted their dream becoming reality. Little did I know the dream, the vision that God was about to show Martha and me. But the agony preceded the ecstasy. A family member appeared at my side in the wings. I thought how odd that she was there at 9:00 AM. Why wasn't she at her work? She said that she was there just to watch the program with me.

After the accolades, she said, "Let's walk out to our cars." I knew something was wrong. The walk through the parking lot seemed to take days. What has happened now? Why doesn't she just tell me? Just say it? We reached my car at last. "Ronnie just called. He found Martha unconscious and bleeding in the bathroom. They rushed her to the hospital, critically ill. Martha is asking for you. You need to go immediately."

A bomb exploded within me. My world was once again collapsing before my eyes. I couldn't lose Martha. Not another sacrifice. Wasn't there a ram in the thicket for Martha?

And Abraham lifted up his eyes, and looked,
and saw behind him a ram caught in a thicket
by his horns: and Abraham went and took the ram,
and offered him up for a burnt offering
instead of his son. Genesis 22:13

No more, God, no more.

The four hour drive to Augusta was another turning point in my life. As I cried to and pleaded with God, begging Him not to take her away from me, I promised Him that I would go and do and be whatever He wanted. He knew that I would do whatever He said. Had I not walked out His commands to go to the Seminary, to North Main Baptist Church, to Columbus High and Trinity United Methodist Church? Once again, I was willing to go or stay or whatever, but please, this time with Martha.

As I raced down the hall of the St Josephs' second floor, a nurse approached me, "Are you Martha Young's sister from Phenix City? She's been waiting for you." As I entered the Nuclear Medicine suite, my heart was crushed as I saw her lying, frail, ashen and colorless on a gray steel table. The coldness of the room plus the unfamiliar machines looming over and around Martha added to the surreal atmosphere. She reached for me, and we once again held each other.

Her weakened voiced whispered, "I'm alright now. You're here."

"Yes, I'm here. Everything will be alright." But I knew it wasn't.

As they were taking her to a telemetry unit, I was emotionally torn. My spirit told me that I could no longer go back into our room - the safety of our childhood. I had learned too much from the Enneagram, from my divorce, to go back. I had chosen to no longer retreat from the battles of life, but my emotions wanted to cover and protect Martha in the safety of our room. The internal conflict raged between my Divine Image, who knew to trust and walk out His plan for us, and my strong personality, who wanted to retreat and cover. I walked the halls until I let go and reached out by phone to a friend. I needed help.

Two are better than one; for if they fall, the one will lift up his fellow...Ecclesiastes 4: 9, 10

Reaching out - even over the phone - was a huge step for me. Through talking out my survival strategy of withdrawing, I let down my defense systems enough to hear what this dear friend said to me. "You must not turn back around and go into your childhood room. You have come too far for that. Stay centered. In God's strength, you will walk back in that room of reality and say - **no more**."

Reoriented by the testimony of that witness, I knew that now was the time to bring Martha out with me. No longer would I allow us to go back into our room. Yes, I had learned too much from the Enneagram, too much from my divorce, from my tearing down of strongholds. I would no longer retreat from the battles of life. Now I could and would bring Martha out with me. I had promised God and, at last, I was strong enough - centered in Him - to follow through!

When I returned to the telemetry unit about 2:00 AM, she said, "Where have you been?" I told her I had been pacing the halls and talking with a friend on the phone. She said, "That's okay. You're here, and we are back in our room, safe now aren't we?"

"Yes, Martha, but we cannot stay here. We must be strong and courageous enough to walk out. We are now in control and no longer vulnerable. We must go from 'no more' to 'much more' starting right now, this very morning. He will lead us and tell us what to say and do. Let's find something to write on."

I felt the Power of the Universe picking us up, setting our feet on a solid rock and establishing our goings, giving us a new song to sing, a new mission, a new direction on our journey.

I waited patiently for the Lord, and He inclined unto me and heard my cry. He brought me up also out of a horrible pit, out of a miry clay, and set my feet upon a rock, and established my goings.

And He has put a new song in my mouth, even

praise unto our God; many shall see it, and fear,

and shall trust in the Lord.

Psalm 40: 1-3

During the next three hours, *Much, Much More* was born as we became partners, this time professionally as well as personally - motivated and mobilized to take our message to the masses, to all that God places before us.

Much, Much More

- **You Already Have It**
- **Rediscover It**
- **Choose to Develop It**
- **Share It**

The next few days were a mountaintop experience. We were bathed in His Spirit as He radiated His Love in and through us. The team of doctors never found the source of the internal bleeding that caused the problem. We walk daily not knowing if or when it might reoccur. What we do know is that we are "Safe in His Hand, Within His Plan".

When I was a child, I spoke as a child, I understood as a child, I thought as a child: but when I became a man, I put away childish things. For

we now see through a glass darkly (mirror);
but then face to face; now I know in part
but then shall I know as also I am known.
I Corinthians 13: 11, 12

God's little girls were growing up!

You Already Have It!

Awaken to Your Spirit

- Acknowledge the existence of your spirit who lives in the Secret Sanctuary of your Soul.

- Celebrate the beauty and authenticity of Spirit who is the Image of God.

- "I will give thanks to Thee, for I am fearfully and wonderfully made." Psalms 139:14

Chapter 6

<u>The Second Garden</u>

"The Way ... The Garden of Gethsemane"

And the Word was made flesh, and dwelt among us,
(and we beheld His glory, the glory as of the only
begotten of the Father) full of grace and truth.

John 1: 14

Jesus, the I Am that I Am of Exodus, took
on our human form, experienced our humanness, in
order to show us the Way. Satan tempted Jesus in
the wilderness, but He did not turn.

And Jesus answering said unto him, It is said,
Thou shalt not tempt the Lord thy God.
And when the devil had ended all the temptation, he
departed from Him for a season.
And Jesus returned in the power of the Spirit.

Luke 4:12-14

He didn't take on survival strategies to
get others to love Him, like we do, clothed in
our personalities - trying to be more perfect, or
more helpful, or more successful, etc.. Although
fully human, Jesus remained centered, focused,
manifesting God's Divine Image given to us in

the beginning:

> I am the Light…
>
> I am the Bread…
>
> I am the Living Water…
>
> I am the Way…
>
> I am the Truth…
>
> I am the Door…
>
> I am the Life…
>
> I am the Good Shepherd…
>
> I am the Vine.

He was unaffected by the *voices* of man as He walked out "The Way, The Truth and The Life".

Jesus saith unto him, I am the way, the truth, and the life: no man comes unto the Father, but by me.

John 14: 6

Satan, the government and religious groups tried to turn Him from the Father by temptation, entrapment, trickery, the promise of earthly power and finally the threat of death. The Good News is that in the Second Garden, Gethsemane, Jesus redeemed us by exemplifying **The Way** to return to wholeness, to Union with God, to the Divine Oneness of the First Garden - *by Re-Turning.*

STOP

Jesus withdrew, **focused**, and connected.

And He was withdrawn from them...

And kneeled down and prayed. Luke 22: 41

LOOK

He was **fully aware** of the sacrifice to come and inner conflict.

This is My Body which is given for you.

This is My Blood which is shed for you.

Luke 22: 19, 20

REVISIT

He **spoke** with the Father, expressing resistance to the original plan because He had 'put on' our sins – our personalities looking for another way.

Father if Thou be willing, remove this cup from Me:

nevertheless, not My will but Thine be done.

Luke 22: 42

SENSE IT

He sweated drops of blood as He allowed the chaos resulting from the worldly motivations, or fixations, of our Egos and Personalities.

And being in agony, He prayed more earnestly and

His sweat was as it were great drops of blood

falling down to the ground.

Luke 23: 44

LET IT HURT

He walked it out on the cross.

Who for the joy that was set before Him endured

the cross despising the shame.

Hebrews 12: 2

REORIENT

He gave up the resistant breath of man's Ego and committed His Spirit into the Hand of the Father.

*And when **Jesus cried with a loud voice**, He said,*

Father into Thy hands I commend My spirit: and

*having said thus, **He gave up** the ghost. Luke 23: 46*

RESTORE

He **became One with the God-Head**, reconnecting the Trinity providing the change in direction for us.

That they all may be One; as Thou, Father, art in

me, and I in Thee, that they also may be One in us:

that the world may believe that

Thou has sent Me. John 17: 21

SHARE IT

He **appeared** to the women and Disciples and **walked** among many for 40 days, talking to them about the Kingdom of God, The Indwelling Eternal Presence.

To whom also He showed Himself alive after His

passion by many infallible proofs, being seen of

them forty days, and
speaking of the things pertaining to
the Kingdom of God. Acts 1: 3

REVIVAL

Modeling the Way of the **pulling down** of our Personalities' **strongholds,** He gives us the Freedom to *Dance the Dance of our Deliverance!*
*For the weapons of our warfare are not carnal, but mighty through God to the **pulling down of strong holds**: Casting down imaginations and every high thing that exalts itself against the knowledge of God and bringing into captivity every thought to the obedience of Christ.*
II Corinthians 10: 4, 5
Let them praise His name in dance.
Psalms 149: 3

So we see that the more we try, the more frustrated we become, the more tangled up in the web of illusions we find ourselves with seemingly no way out! We will always wear parts of our False Selves, our Personalities, our hats to some extent, but we no longer have to be bound by them. Paul again proclaims the Truth that sets us free:

I (Personality) *am crucified with Christ: nevertheless, I* (Divine Image) *live: yet not I but Christ lives in me: and the life which I now live in the flesh I live by the faith of the Son of God, who loved me, and gave Himself for me.*

Galatians 2:20

Chapter 7

Our Second Garden

"His Way Becomes Our Way"

By following the example of Jesus, by letting go, we allow the Truth to set us free.

STOP

Cease striving. This in itself will take effort in our breakneck pace of living. Breathe deeply and focus your thoughts on Him. Remember, the Holy Spirit breathes life into you. Expect Him to walk you through the Way. Most people totally disregard the transforming power of the breath. The oxygen in the blood travels through you and touches every part of your body as it picks up all impurities expelling it through the breath. You can control your breathing thereby being in control of any situation. You've all heard the phrase, "Take a deep breath and count to ten." Think about it – it works. **You Already Have It.**

Be still and know that I am God: I will be exalted among the heathen, I will be exalted in the earth.

Psalm 46: 10

I waited patiently for the Lord; and He inclined unto me. Psalms 40: 1

LOOK

Focus on the Kingdom. Center down.

Seek ye first the Kingdom of God and His right-

eousness. Matthew 6: 33

Search me, O God, and know my heart:

Try me, and know my thoughts.

Psalms 139: 23

Awareness

Wake up! Look around you. Trust yourself to see what is really happening. Discard old glasses with wrong prescriptions that distort your view of reality and leave you in fear. What is fear anyway except False Evidence Assumed Real! **The Truth is that the King of the universe is within you!**

Now why do you cry out aloud?

Is there no king in you? Is your Counselor

(the Holy Spirit) *perished? Micah 4: 9*

Put on the lens corrected by the cross. You no longer have to view the world through the eyes of a vulnerable child. Now in the Spirit of Truth you can see what is happening in the present and trust that you can correctly assess and deal with any situation strong, filled with power, love and a sound mind.

For God has not given us a spirit of fear,

but of power and of love and of a sound mind.

II Timothy 1: 7

102

It is Jesus who tells us where to look,

Neither shall they say, Look here! Look there!

For behold, The Kingdom of God is within you.

Luke 17: 21

REVISIT

Acknowledge the pain of the past.

Childhood - the beginning of coverings. A genetic basis for personality along with our relationships with our parents, or significant others, powerfully mold and define our personalities. How we perceive the actions of others towards us, not necessarily the actions themselves, become the fuel for our focus of attention and fundamental motivations - to our very sense of self. Basically, how we feel about ourselves is determined by how we think others feel and think about us! This perception - right or wrong - gives rise to our basic fears and resulting basic desires. As children, we create whatever defense systems are necessary to make us feel safe in situations in which we are vulnerable.[10]

These defensive mechanisms worked so well they became habitual behavior patterns. For example, in my case, I withdraw from conflict or tried to fix every difficult situation. Others may go

---

[10] Riso, Don Richard, with Russ Hudson. Personality Types. New York: Houghton Mifflin Company, 1996.

into a rage. Still others may cry. Have you ever said, "I don't know why I acted like that"? Or have you ever been afraid that you would blow in a stressful situation? Or thought, "Where in the world are they coming from?" What happens in the present is constantly being invaded by the past. It's the games we play, the familiar dress we put on. In moments of stress, we regress into our past and put on "known" defensive behaviors that were constructed to protect us from interactions we were too young to integrate or interpret. Unfortunately, these reactions are not appropriate to present situations.[11]

In other words, the child within us is responding to trigger words that bring on a repeated childhood behavior – acting out. The stressful situation is no longer experienced in the present but rather as it was in the past. These resulting behaviors reappear automatically in response to trigger words. Trigger words are words or phrases heard early in life that originally created the defensive mechanisms.

"You're driving me crazy."

"You'll never amount to anything."

"You're stupid."

"You've done it again."

"Why can't you be like _____?"

---

[11] *Ibid.*

"You're so lazy."

The repetitive defensive patterns of behavior are built brick by brick, creating a façade that we project to the world covering our Divine Image. Just as Eve needed covering when she listened to the outside voice and turned, we also create our coverings or masks - our personalities. When we turn to receive our worth and value from the deceptive voices of the world, we, like Eve, eat the fruit of frustration, guilt, shame, fear, anxiety, anger, depression and on and on.

We now know that we have taken the first step toward understanding the source of our inner struggle - the same struggle Paul spoke of in Romans 7. We are not alone.

Does this mean that all our childhood memories are painful ones? Absolutely not! Martha and I have many wonderful, delightful memories filled with love and family. These serve us well and help us relate in healthy ways to our environments most of the time. In fact, as we revisit our childhood let's first re-experience our good memories.

SENSE IT

The Past - Recall your first good memory.

Where are you?

How old are you?

Recall the situation through your senses: Taste, Smell, Hearing, Touch, Sight

Who else was there?

What are the resulting feelings you have now?

Now recall your first difficult recurring memory.

Where are you?

How old are you?

Recall the situation through your senses: Taste, Smell, Hearing, Touch, Sight.

Who else was there?

Who was in charge?

Who was vulnerable?

Who hurt you, conditioned you, and disconnected you with your spirit?

What are the resulting feelings you have now?

The Present

Who is still in charge?

Who is still vulnerable?

Who are you **allowing** it to hurt you, condition you, and disconnect you from your spirit?

LET IT HURT

Experience the pain.

Instead of resisting the emotional pain associated with your difficult memory, take time to let it hurt.

In the midst of our busy lives,

Time races on...

No time to grieve,

No time to cry,

No time to die,

No time to ask

...Why?[12]

But now is that needed set-apart time. As Jesus took time in the Garden to agonize, you can take time to grieve, to cry, to die to the pain, and it's okay to ask why. It takes time to be whole.

Be compassionate with yourself. You may have suffered terrible abuse in your childhood that left you with a victim orientation in life. You may unconsciously expect and allow another person to abuse you. Emotional abuse can be as devastating as physical abuse. Alcoholism, divorce, death of a parent, sibling or another significant loved one(s), mental, emotional, physical or sexual abuse, physical abnormalities, major illnesses and on and on, must be brought up, experienced, then exposed to God's healing Light. Be aware that *everyone* you meet has some hurt tucked away. Ironically, the person or people who hurt you were reacting to their own hidden pains by projecting them on you. Likewise, you have probably unintentionally hurt a

---

12 Grimes, Dixie Land, "Why?", 1996.

loved one, perpetuating the destructive cycle. You are not alone or different. The greatest gift you can give your children - besides introducing them to Christ - is to **break these deadly patterns!** Remember: Deadly family secrets are the real killers.

Visualize.

Visualize Jesus taking you into His arms and holding you until you can release the pain. This is a vital step towards becoming "holy" - whole and complete. We all have emotional baggage. If a person denies it, he/she has just buried it so deeply that he/she either can't bring it up or doesn't want to share it. It is time to unload. Hopefully, you already have a friend you can trust to walk with you through this experience. They just need to listen without judgment or solutions. Friends like Job had, you don't need!

If not, seek out someone. Ask God specifically and expectantly to guide you to this special person. He may just bring that person to your front door!

You may have to go through this process two or three times. Remember God allowed His saints to complain, even whine - Elijah under the Juniper tree, Job, Noah, the impotent man by the pool, etc. He patiently listened, provided for their immediate needs *then* expected them *to get up* and *go* about their mission. Just don't allow it to become a habitual pattern. This is unloading, not multiplying the pain! You are no longer a vulnerable child. *You are an adult with choices.* Therefore, **Choose.**

Choose to be well, whole, complete.

Wilt thou be made whole? John 5:6

Accept healing.

Rise, take up thy bed and walk! John 5: 8

Pick yourself up, dust yourself off and start all over again!

REORIENT

Give it up! Take off your defense systems, your survival strategies. For example, I had to let go of my withdrawing response to conflict and stop my compulsion to 'fix' everything and everybody. This is the hardest part. Rip off that outer garment that you have woven to protect your vulnerable inner Spirit. This garment, no matter how lovely it appears to the world, hides your true gifts and the aspect of Christ that reflects God's Image! When you look into the mirror every morning, what do you see - a mask you put on 'to make it' through the day? Or do you see God's reflection - His

Image - radiating His love? Pull down those
strongholds! Lay aside those weights.

Let us lay aside every weight (defensive strategies),
and the sin (separation from God's Image) *that so*
easily besets us and let us run the race that is set
before us. Hebrews 12: 1

We must also let go of attitudes and attachments that anchor us to the world. Do you want to
let go in order to find happiness? Do you think that if
you follow Christ, He will reward you with peace
and prosperity via financial security? You may want
God to fix a relationship. Be totally honest. What are
the desires of your heart? Why are you seeking the
Lord? Remember how I was trying to follow His
Word, working as hard as I could to do things correctly so that He would justify my life. "If You don't
honor my desire to follow You by restoring my
family, my whole life will be a joke." Sounds like a
scene from Job, doesn't it? I thank God that He saw
beyond that childlike attitude to my deepest need and
desire - to be in union with Him. My *garden event*
forced me to *let go* so that I could *grow up* in Him.

RESTORE

Restoring your relationship with God
requires a refocusing or a centering down in Him. It

is time to grow up. We are to come to Him as little children, but we are to grow up in Him as we become His Body in order to minister in His Spirit to this dark and difficult world. Children are constantly wanting their needs met. Paul labored with childish followers in I Corinthians 3: 1-23.

I have fed you with milk and not with meat...

for you are carnal; for among you is

envying, strife, divisions. I Corinthians 3: 2, 3

They were behaving like immature children, all seeking to get what they wanted. They were also lifting up certain leaders.

For while one says,

I am of Paul; and another,

I am of Apollos.I Corinthians 3: 4

Instead of looking unto Jesus, the author and finisher of their faith, they were looking to men and also dividing their allegiances between them. All too often we look to others - our spouse, loved ones, or friends to give us love, self-confidence, approval, self-esteem, etc. If or when they don't, we get angry, become depressed and blame them for our problems. The first giant step in **growing up** is awareness - seeing people and situations as they really are, not what we want them to be in order to satisfy our needs. A spiritually and emotionally mature adult doesn't go around trying to get love from the outside. That leads to looking for love in all the wrong places **and people**! He/she has all the love that is needed because he/she is connected to the Source of Love. **Therefore, growing up is just re-connecting to the Source of all life!** It's like having the most beautiful and expensive lamp in the world and not plugging it into an electrical socket!

Does that mean that you will be alone? No, that is another childish fear. Being restored in and reconnected to God, you will be Divinely interconnected - abiding in the Body of Christ, receiving all the love, support, nourishment and life you will ever need or desire. When we are abiding in the Spirit of Truth, He becomes our desire. He becomes our life.

I (Jesus) *am the true vine and my Father* (God), *the husbandman...Abide in Me and I in you...He that abides in Me and I in him, the same brings forth much fruit. If you abide in Me and my words abide in you, ask what you will and it shall be done unto you.*

John 14: 1, 4, 5, 7

SHARE IT

As our relationship with God is restored, He energizes us with power to go and share the good news.

All power is given unto me in heaven and in earth,
Go ye, therefore, and teach all nations,
baptizing them in the name of the Father
and of the Son and of the Holy Ghost.
Teaching them to observe all things
whatsoever I have commanded you; and, lo,
I am with you always, even unto the ends of the
earth. Matthew 28: 19, 20

Our work becomes His work. We become fishers of men.

Come after me and
I will make you fishers of men. Mark 1: 17
Jesus said unto Peter, Feed my sheep. John 21: 17

Your life becomes His life. Your desire is to allow Him to live and move and have His Being in and through you, no matter what or where.

When you were young, you clothed yourself and
walked where you would, but when you are old, you
shall stretch forth your hands and another shall
clothe you and carry you where you would not go.
Follow me. John 21:18, 19

It may be anywhere, anytime, to anyone.

I am ready to preach the gospel to you that are in Rome... For I am not ashamed of the gospel of Christ. For it is the power of God unto salvation to everyone that believes; to the Jew first, and also to the Greek. ...The just shall live by faith. Romans 1:15, 16

REVIVAL

Revival leads to new life in the Third Garden ...the Eternal Now.

Chapter 8

<u>The Third Garden</u>

"Our Foretaste of Eternal Glory"

Behold, the tabernacle of God is with men, and He will dwell with them, and they shall be His people, and God Himself shall be with them and be their God.

Revelation 21: 3

So we now see the Truth. We already have the love we are desperately seeking. It does not come from the outside, from others. It is within us, where the Source of Love abides, in our Center, our inner sanctuary, our Holy of Holies.

Living from the inside that's
where I want to be.
Reaching out to others
Who will find their way through me.
Love is the answer, His love is the key.
Love will tear the walls down that
imprison you and me.[13]

Hear me[14], wherever you are in your journey, the Love that is the answer - that will tear

---

[13] Grimes, Dixie Land, "Living From the Inside", 1996.
[14] Matthew 11:15.

down the walls that imprison you and me - is not the love we receive or don't receive from others. That love is **conditional**. It is Love Himself, the Love that created us in His image. His Love is unconditional, and it is within us! **You already have it!**

We see **it** as Jesus, from the cross, looked down on His murderers and said,

Father, forgive them, for they know not what they
do. Luke 23: 34

We see **it** as He rescues the adulterous woman, saying,

They say unto Him 'Master, this woman was taken
in adultery, in the very act.'
When Jesus had lifted up Himself, and saw none
but the woman, He said unto her,
'Woman, where are your accusers?...
...Neither do I condemn thee:
go and sin no more." John 8: 4,10,11

We see **it** as He does not retaliate or rail an "I told you so!" at Peter after he rejected Him, but asked if Peter loved Him and then trusted Peter to feed His sheep.

So when they had dined, Jesus said to Simon Peter,
Simon, son of Jonas, Do you love me more than
these? He saith unto Him, Yes, Lord; You know that

I love Thee.
He said unto him, Feed My lambs.
He said to him again the second time, Simon, son of
Jonas, Do you love Me? He said unto Him,
Yes, Lord; You know that I love You.
He said unto him, Feed My sheep.
He said unto him the third time, Simon, son of
Jonas, Do you love Me? Peter was grieved
because He said unto him the third time, Do you
love Me? And he said unto Him, Lord, You know
all things; You know that I love You. Jesus said
unto him, Feed My Sheep.
John 21: 15-17

We see **it** with Jesus sharing the first universal call with the woman at the well - a woman of ill repute!

Woman, believe Me. The hour comes when you
shall neither in this mountain nor yet at Jerusalem,
worship the Father. The hour comes, and now is,
when the true worshippers shall worship
the Father in Spirit and in Truth.
John 4: 7-26

We see **it** as Jesus calls you and me to Re-Turn to Him, to trust Him and to listen only to Him. His words of love free and affirm us. They empower us to open to the world to allow His Love

to flow as a river of living water through us to a dry
and parched land.

But whosoever drinks of the water that I shall give
him shall never thirst; but the water that I shall
give him shall be in him a well of water spring up
into everlasting life. John 4: 14

We are already who we need to be. We are
and have always been the Image of the great I AM.
We are the image, the picture of "I AM THAT I
AM".

And God said unto Moses, I AM THAT I AM: and
He said, Thus shall you say unto the
children of Israel, I AM has sent me unto you.
Exodus 3: 14

Chapter 9

Our Third Garden

"Union With God - Our Eternal Now"

So the Way to restoration in our Third Garden, to the Source of Love, is as simple as releasing instead of resisting. By taking off our masks, our emotional armor, and not trying so hard, we can begin to trust that we are all that we need to be. By Re-Turning or turning around, we find that we are already home. The Kingdom of God is not on the outside. The Kingdom of God is within you.

The Kingdom of God comes not with observation; neither shall they say, 'Look here! Or, Look there!' For, behold, the Kingdom of God is within you.

Luke 17: 20, 21

As the Psalmist celebrates, we join the unending chorus, we are fearfully and wonderfully made, the Divine expression of Himself, adorned with special gifts and qualities of God.

I will praise You; for I am fearfully and wonderfully made: marvelous are Your works; and that my soul knows right well.

Psalms 139: 14

As we Re-Turn to the innocence of trust, let us question not our existence. We need not be aware of our past nor future, for we can live in the Divine present, delighting in each unfolding moment as we observe life from our inner Holy of Holies, the Dwelling place of God. Then and only then will each day be an adventure. Coming from the Source of Love, we are re-connected, whole, at One with the Divine.

*That they all may be One; as You, Father, are in me, and I am in You, that they also may be One in us: that the world may believe that You have sent me. And the glory which You gave me I have given to them; that they may be **One**, even as we are **One**. **I in them, and You in me**, that they may be made perfect* (mature - grown-up) *in **One**; and that the world may know that You have sent me and have loved them, as You have loved me.*

John 17: 21-23

Excitedly, we began to Re-Orient, Re-Focus from the outside to the inside, knowing that from such an orientation we can be a part of our stimulating, environment; but this time, we know, as Jesus showed us, that **we are in the world but not of it.**

They are not of the world, even as I am not of the world. John 17: 16

120

We are now freed from the vice of fleeting time to become part of the Third Garden, the Eternal Now. Living in the Divine Present, we experience God's perspective,

One day is with the Lord as a thousand years,

and a thousand years as one day.

II Peter 3: 8

We trust that we are where we need to be and when we need to be there. In Divine confidence, therefore, we boldly go forth in the liberating faith that we are finally free to be all we are designed to be.

Living from the inside,

That's where I want to be,

Reaching out to others who will find

their way through me.

Love is the answer, His love is the key.

Love will tear the walls down that imprison

you and me.[15]

Revival frees us to dance

the Dance of our Deliverance!

Then and only then, we will have a foretaste of the Eternal Perfect Garden of Revelation 22, where there is no need for anything, for God is the Source of everything. Today we can know a fore-

---

[15] Grimes, Dixie Land, "Living From the Inside", 1998.

taste of this Eternal Garden by abiding in Christ.
Only then will we know the transforming power of
the Spirit of Truth.

And all of us, as with unveiled faces (no need for
covering) reflecting as a mirror the glory of the
Lord, are transformed into the same image from
glory to glory, even as from the Lord the Spirit.
II Corinthians 3: 18

We all have Power. We can now reach out
and touch others allowing them to release their
Power. Share His Power! Share His Light coming
from your Center, your Holy of Holies. Light your
candle then use your flame to light another's. Light
the world one candle at a time. It works! It really
works!

We are now finally, faithfully, willing to be all we
were designed to be: Free to be me!

"Free to be me...to become
all I was created to be."

"For they that wait upon the
Lord shall mount up with
wings as eagles."
Isaiah 40:31

Chapter 10

<u>Daily Spiritual Exercise</u>

"My Desire For You"

Dear Sister or Brother in Christ,

You are the Image of God - Divinely made to fellowship with Him and to carry His message of love and life to others. It is exciting but not surprising that you are feeling a desire to be closer to God, because the Bible says that He is drawing you to Himself. You are responding to His call to you! He loves you and wants to enjoy a more intimate relationship with you. Isn't that wonderful? Thank you for allowing me to show you His Good News about you in His Word.

When you first get up in the morning, look in the mirror and see God's reflection, His creation - You. If your feelings tell you otherwise, be aware that those are feelings, generated by chemicals in your body, responding to negative input. God tells you how much He loves you, how wonderful you are and what plans He has for you.

A. Your part is to daily:

   1. Take in His Word.

   2. Believe what His Word says.

3. Experience His Presence.

4. Practice walking out His Presence.

5. Share His Presence!

I know this is true because I have lived it and SO CAN YOU!

B. Remember the two rules Jesus gave us in Mark 12: 30, 31:

1. You shall love the Lord thy God with all your heart, with all your soul and with all your mind and with all thy strength.

2. You shall love your neighbor as thyself.

C. 'Eat' as you choose to believe these Scriptures every day and you will be 'Spiritually Fit'.

1. Genesis 1:26: "And God said, Let us make man in our own image, after our own likeness." You are God's image!

2. Genesis 32: 24-28: "Jacob said, 'I will not let you go except you bless me.'" Jacob would not let God go until He blessed him. Do not let God go until He gives you all you want of Him. Remember that Jacob became Israel! (Genesis 35:10,11)

3. Deuteronomy 8: 3: "…Man does not live by bread alone, but by every Word that proceeds out of the mouth of the Lord does man live."

4. Deuteronomy 20: 3, 4: "...the Lord your God is He that goes with you, to fight for you against your enemies." (Stress, depression, fears, anxiety, inertia - all the emotions that plague us.) He will fight all your battles with you.

5. Psalms 40: 1-4: "He has brought me out of an horrid pit, out of the miry clay and set my feet upon a solid rock and established my goings." He will empower you.

6. Psalms 42: 1-5: "As the hart pants after the water brooks, so pants my soul after You, O my soul. Hope in God." You desire Him, too. Wonderful!

7. Psalms 139: 17, 18: "How precious are Your thoughts unto me, O God! How great is the sum of them!" He thinks of you.

8. Isaiah 55: 8,11,12: "For you will go out with joy and go forth with peace: the mountains and the hills shall break forth with singing, and all the trees of the fields shall clap their hands." Even nature rejoices over you.

9. Jeremiah 29: 11: "I know the thoughts I have toward you, says the Lord: thoughts of peace and not of evil, to give you an

expected end.... And you will seek me and find me when you shall seek me with all your heart." He is your future and your hope.

10. Jeremiah 31: 3: "The Lord appeared unto me saying, Yes, I have loved thee with an everlasting love; therefore, with loving kindness I have drawn thee." He woos you.

11. Jeremiah 31: 33: "I will put my law in their inward parts and write it on their hearts and will be their God and they shall be my people." He connects with you intimately.

12. Luke 17: 21: "...the Kingdom of God is within you..." He lives in you.

13. John 15: 16: "You have not chosen me; but I have chosen you, and ordained you that you should go and bring forth fruit, and that your fruit should remain: that whatsoever you shall ask of the Father in my name, He may give it to you." You are chosen and have a specific purpose.

14. John 15: 4: "Abide in Me and I in you." You and God are One.

15. John 17: 23: "I in them, and Thou in me, that they may be perfect (mature) in one; and that the world may know that Thou has

sent me and has loved them as Thou has loved Me." He loves you as much as He loves Jesus.

16. John 3: 16: "For God so loved the world that He gave His only begotten Son, that whosoever believes on Him shall be saved." God loves you this much.

> Love,
>
> Dixie

Restoring

"*I will restore to you the years that the locust has eaten...and my people will never be ashamed.*"

Joel 2:25 & 27

- Choose To Be Free!
- Choose To Be Present!
- Choose To Experience Un-conditioned Love!
- Choose To Accept Un-conditioned Love!

Prayer of Restoration

With our hearts united in His love, we pray:

Holy Father, Creator of the universe,

As the Psalmist celebrates, we join the unending chorus that we are fearfully and wonderfully made, the Divine expression of Himself, adorned with special gifts and qualities of God.

When You created us in Your Divine Image, You gave us all that we will ever need. But we, like Adam and Eve, have turned from You and listened to voices of the world. We, too, have tasted the fruit of deception and dishonor, resulting in guilt, shame and blame.

Forgive us for turning from You and listening to the voices of the world.

Return our hearts to You by the power of Your Holy Spirit.

Refresh our minds that we may reclaim the truth that our every need has already been met through the power and unconditional love that is within us in Jesus Christ.

Refocus our eyes that through our worship, we may see the truth You have for each one of us personally and for all of us as the Body of Christ.

Empower us to share this truth in our homes, our churches, our schools, our professions, our government - in all of our relationships, not only where we live, but also throughout our country and our challenging world.

We ask with great expectation and joy in the name of Jesus Christ, our Savior and Lord.

Amen

Share It

- Free To Be Present

- Free To Be Vulnerable

- Free To Engage in Life

- Free to Delight in the
  Dance of Your
  Deliverance!

Songs Given in the Night
Isaiah 30:29

"HOW DO I SEE YOU"
DIXIE LAND GRIMES

DUET

VERSE

How can I go on now that you know me?
Now that you know who I am?
Darkness surrounds me and doubt walls me in.
Fear overwhelms me, I'm broken, my friend.

CHORUS

How do I see you, with eyes open wide?
How do I see you, There's no need to hide.
I'm blinded by love, for my soul is set free,
I'm blinded by love now it's easy to see,
How do I see you? As He sees me.

VERSE

How did I get here and where do I go?
I do not know where I am.

Let go of all that keeps you from me.
All that would bind you and won't set you free.

CHORUS

VERSE

How did we get here and where do we go?
I need to know why I am.

Open yourself now His love sets you free.
Without the shadows you're all you can be.

133

"LIVING FROM THE INSIDE"
DIXIE LAND GRIMES

Verse

Searching for direction, which way should I go?
Can anyone show me? Does anybody know?
The way seems so distant and yet so very near...
Questions seem to haunt me, but answers aren't so clear.

I'm looking for a way now to fill an empty hole,
All the world has given just covered up my soul.
Why have I run so when I didn't need to roam?
Blocking inner vision that keeps me from home,

Chorus

Living from the inside, that's where I want to be,
Reaching out to others who will learn the way through me.
Love is the answer, His Love is the key,
Love will break the walls down that imprison you and me.

Verse

Looking for the answers, screening as I run.
He calls me to listen, "The battle has been won."
I'm opening the door now, ready to be free.
He had all the answers just waiting there for me.

Chorus

Living from the inside, that's where I want to be,
Reaching out to others who will learn the way through me.
Love is the answer, His Love is the key,
Love will break the walls down that imprison you and me.

"WHY, GOD?"
DIXIE LAND GRIMES

Duet

Why, oh, why, God,
Why am I, God, who I am?
Who do You think I am?
Who do You want me to be?

Come to Me.
I'm the Great I Am.
You are Who I Am.
We are One.

Searching for me,
Reaching for Thee.
Am I only in my mind?
Who will I find?

Come to me.
I'm waiting for Thee.
Abide in Me.
Love through Me.

Because of My Son,
We are One.

Bibliography

As God has revealed so much about our journey through their thoughts and works, we are indebted to all these authors. We highly recommend the following books, gratefully acknowledging that their input is throughout our book.

Aspell, Dee Dee & Patrick. *"Enneagram Transparencies for Christian Application"*. San Antonio, TX: Lifewings, Ltd., 1995.

_____. *Profiles Of The Enneagram: Ways of Coming Home to Yourself.* San Antonio, TX: Lifewings, Ltd., 1994.

Carroll, Joseph S. *How To Worship Jesus Christ.* Tennessee: Riverside Press, 1994.

Chambers, Oswald. *Conformed to His Image.* Michigan: Zondervan Publishing House, 1985.

Guyon, Jeanne. *Union With God.* Maine: Christian Books, 1981.

Hurley, Kathleen, and Theodore Dobson. *My Best Self.* New York: HarperCollins Publishers, 1993.

Hurley, Kathleen, and Theodore Donson. *Discover Your Soul Potential.* Lakewood, CO: WindWalker Press, 2000.

Kelly, Thomas R. *A Testament of Devotion.* New York: Harper & Row, 1941.

Keirsey, David, and Marilyn Bates. *Please Understand Me.* Del Mar, California.: Prometheus Nemesis Books, 1978.

Kierkegaard, Soren. *Christian Discourses.* Translated by Walter Lowie, Cambridge: James Clarke & Co., 1940.

_____. *Stages on Life's Way.* Translated by Walter Lowie, New Jersey: Princeton University Press, 1940.

_____. *The Gospel of Sufferings.* Translated by A. S. Aldworth and W. S. Ferrie. Cambridge: James Clarke & Co., 1955.

Myers, Isabel Briggs, and Peter B. Myers. *Gifts Differing.* Palo Alto, Calif.: Consulting Psychologists Press, Inc., 1980.

Nee, Watchman. *Not I But Christ: Exercise Thyself Unto Godliness.* New York: Christian Fellowship Publishers, Inc., 1974.

Oldham, John M. M.D., and Lois B. Morris. *Personality Self-Portrait; Why You Think, Work, Love, and Act the Way You Do.* New York: Bantam Books, 1991.

Palmer, Helen, and Paul B. Brown. *The Enneagram Advantage.* New York: Harmony Books, 1998.

Riso, Don Richard, with Russ Hudson. *Personality Types.* New York: Houghton Mifflin Company, 1996.

Riso, Don Richard. *Discovering Your Personality Type.* New York: Houghton Mifflin Company, 1992.

Riso, Don Richard, and Russ Hudson. *The Wisdom of the Enneagram.* New York: Bantam Books, 1999.

Tozer, A. W. *Jesus, Author Of Our Faith.* PA.: Christian Publications, 1988.

Available Seminars
Much, Much More Seminars and Consulting

Spiritual
- Discovering Your Spiritual Gifts
- Creating Ministry Teams: Empowering the Body of Christ
- Restoration for Burned-out Ministers
- The Image of God: Re-discovering the Divine Image In You
- A Garden Celebration:
    God's Redemptive Plan as Seen Through the Three
    Biblical Gardens Perspective

Education
- Nine Innovative and Workable Steps to Classroom Management
- Unmasking Behavior: An Innovative Way to Look At An Old Problem
- At Last: A Clear View of Why Teachers Act and React The Way They Do
- Discovery and Development of Effective Administrative Leadership

Business
- Nine Ways of Improving the Health of Your Practice
- The Domino Effect
- Nine Steps Toward Personnel Empowerment Rather Than Personnel Management
- Empower Your Practice by Empowering Your People

For further information and scheduling, please contact:

Dixie Land Grimes * 2755 Wintergreen Court
Phenix City, AL 36867 * (334) 291-9884
E-Mail: angelscry2@msn.com
Martha Land Young * 7207 Holland Place NW
Lawrenceville, GA 30043 * (678) 985-1844
E-Mail: MarthaLand@aol.com

Dixie Land Grimes - Ordained Southern Baptist Minister, Educator and Musician, Reverend Grimes has a BA in Music Education, University of South Carolina, and a Masters Degree in Music, Southwestern Baptist Theological Seminary, Fort Worth, Texas. She teaches music in Muscogee County School District, Columbus, Georgia, where she is also a Teacher Support Specialist and Staff Development Instructor and Facilitator. Dixie and Martha lead seminars in churches, school districts and businesses.

Martha Land Young As an Ophthalmic Administrator for 20 years, Martha endeavored to nurture and develop the individuals God placed under her authority. Martha combined her professional skills with her Christian beliefs and created an environment in which each individual could blossom which brings into being a dynamic team. In Martha's capacity as a consultant and a presenter, she shares how to affirm and develop all employees in an organization.

NOTES

[1] Grimes, Dixie Land. "Living From the Inside", 1996.

[2] *Ibid.*

[3] *Ibid.*

[4] Grimes, Dixie Land. "Letting Go", 1998.

[5] Grimes, Dixie Land. "Living From the Inside", 1997.

[6] Genesis 3, KJV.

[7] Psalms 139:14.

[8] Romans 7: 14-24.

[9] Palmer, Helen, and Paul B. Brown. *The Enneagram Advantage.* New York: Harmony Books, 1998.

[10] Riso, Don Richard, with Russ Hudson. Personality Types. New York; Houghton Mifflin Company, 1996.

[11] *Ibid.*

[12] Grimes, Dixie Land. "Why?", 1996.

[13] Grimes, Dixie Land. "Living From the Inside", 1996.

[14] Matthew 11:15.

[15] Grimes, Dixie Land. "Living From the Inside", 1998.